The Pillars of Islam & Iman

BY
AFTAB SHAHRYAR

Islamic Book Service

© *All Rights Reserved.*

THE PILLARS OF ISLAM & IMAN
by Aftab Shahryar

ISBN: 81-7231-511-2

First Edition: 2004

Published by *Abdul Naeem* for
Islamic Book Service
2241, Kucha Chelan, Darya Ganj, New Delhi-110 002 (India)
Tel.: 23253514, 23265380, 23286551, Fax: 23277913
E-mail: islamic@eth.net & ibsdelhi@del2.vsnl.net.in
Website: www.islamic-india.com

Printed at: *Noida Printing Press,* C-31, Sector-7, Noida (Ghaziabad) U.P.

PREFACE

The Pillars of Islam & Iman is a very brief glimpse, a small window, as it were, looking into an inordinately vast and complex subject. It purports to explain very briefly the body of Islamic knowledge that is basic to the religion of Islam. However, this knowledge, and exposition concerned with every facet of beliefs, worship, values, morals and behaviour, both individual and collective, is so immense that scholars have spent entire life times to master only some part of this knowledge.

At the same time it is necessary and important that all Muslims should understand the basic concepts and obligations that they are required to follow in the light of the guidance offered by the holy Qur'an, and the *Sunnah* of the Prophet (peace & blessings of Allah be with him).

In the early years of the third millennia in spite of great expansion in the frontiers of scientific and technological knowledge, our societies continue to face many crises. In the Islamic view, these problems are fundamentally of a spiritual nature and answers and solutions to these ultimate questions compatible with reason, logic, the realities of the physical universe and with human nature itself can be found in their faith alone. For Islam is, above all, a view of the total Reality, encompassing the existence and attributes of the Creator, the relationship of humans with Him, role and purpose of humans in this world and the relationship between this life and the life of the Hereafter, which puts all that exists into proper perspective and gives balance and direction to the life of humans and their societies.

It is not only non-Muslims who hold a prejudiced view of Islam; sections of Muslims too lead a life of heedlessness and ignorance. This book is a humble attempt to educate all those who seek truth and guidance in Islam.

Aftab Shahryar
New Delhi

CONTENTS

Introduction — vi

Tawheed (Monotheism) — 3

Salat (Prayer) — 21

Siyam (Fasting) — 65

Zakat (Poor-Due) — 79

Hajj (The Annual Pilgrimage to Ka'ba) — 101

Jihad (The All-Round Struggle in the Path of Allah) — 133

Purification of the Body — 143

Purification of the Soul — 167

References — 184

INTRODUCTION

Islam is a worldview, a holistic system with a cardinal framework — articles of faith, basic injunctions, patterns of norms and values. This cardinal framework is eternal. Essentially, the worldview of Islam consists of principles and a matrix of concepts to be found in the Qur'an and *Sunnah*. The principles outline the general rules of behaviour and development and chalk out the general boundaries within which the Muslim civilization has to grow and flourish. The conceptual matrix acts as a standard of measure, a barometer of the Islamicness of a particular situation and it serves as a basis for the elaboration of the worldview of Islam.

The Muslim civilization is not fixed to a particular historic epoch or geographical space than the teachings of Qur'an and the *Sunnah*. The Muslim civilization is a historic continuum. It is a living dynamic civilization. From Medina onwards where the first Islamic community evolved, Islam ceased to be just a religion, or an ethical system or even political system — it became a civilization. And it has continued to be a civilization ever since.

Islam is, above all, a view of total Reality, encompassing the existence and attributes of the Creator, man's relationship with Him, his role and purpose in this world, the relationship between this worldly life and the life of the Hereafter, which places all that exists into proper perspective with a view to giving balance and direction to the life of humans and their societies. Islam is, therefore, seen by some as a total way of life, a complete system, governing all aspects of man's existence, both individual and collective. As a religion it attempts to free the humans from domination by their material and animal aspects and seeks to make them truly human.

The holy prophet (peace & blessings of Allah be with him) is reported to have said that the foremost purpose of his being sent down in this world was of perfecting good morals.

Thus the Islamic mode of prayer is not some kind of a mystic exercise but a means to acquire correct morals and habits and to live righteously, and to believe in and practice these virtues till the end, whatever the changes in their circumstances. Prayer is meant to prohibit obscenity and evil.

Similarly, *Zakat* another pillars of Islam, is a means of purification. The purpose of giving *Zakat* has been mentioned in the Qur'an in the following words:

> O' prophet! Take charity from their property so that it may clean them and purify them (Surah Tauba: 103).

In the same manner fasting, the third pillar of Islam, is a stepping-stone to righteousness. The holy Qur'an asserts: *Fasting has been made compulsory for you... so that you may become righteous. (2: 183).* Likewise the aim of the annual pilgrimage, the *Hajj* is to promote brotherhood amongst the believers and to weaken the love for this world. It is an occasion to reaffirm one's faith in Allah and to renew the pledge to lead a virtuous life.

Therefore, *Salat, Saum, Zakat, Hajj* and other forms of worship purify the hearts of believers, if they nourish noble qualities in those who observe them. But if these forms of worship do not lead to the bonding between the servant and the Lord then these religious exercises are futile.

The holy Qur'an proclaims:

> *Surely, he who appears before his Lord as a criminal, there is Hell for him, in which he will neither die nor will he live.*
>
> *And he who will appear before Him as a faithful, who has performed good deeds — for all such people there are high stations, ever green Paradise, beneath which canals will be flowing and they will dwell therein forever. This is the reward for him who adopts purity.* (Surah Taha: 74-76).

What is Islam?

Islam is the name of the religion revealed through Prophet Muhammad (peace & blessings of Allah be with him) by Allah. The name is explicitly mentioned in the Qur'an that proclaims:

This day have I perfected your religion to you,

completed My favour upon you, and

chosen for you Islam as your religion (Q. V: 4)

Islam is the assertion of the unity of Allah, and faith in the religious precepts revealed by Allah. According to the Qur'an Islam is surrender to Allah. He who submits his will to Allah, obeys all His prophets, is called a Muslim.

The holy Prophet Muhammad (peace & blessings of Allah be with him) is reported to have said that Islam is based on five (things):

First: the *Shahadah* (testimony) *Lailaha Illallah, Muhammadur Rasul-Allah* (there is not deity except Allah, Muhammad is the Messenger of Allah)

Second: *Iqamat as-Salat* (to offer the compulsory congregational prayers properly and punctually).

Third: to give *Zakat* or mandatory charity also referred to as poor-due.

Fourth: to observe fast during the month of *Ramadhan* from dawn to dusk.

Fifth: to perform the annual pilgrimage to the Ka'ba in Makkah known as *Hajj* (obligatory for those who have the means and the strength to do so).

According to a *Hadith* recorded by Imam Muslim on the authority of Hadrat Umar Ibn al-Khattab it is stated as under:

One day while we were sitting with the Messenger of Allah (peace & blessings of Allah be with him) a man suddenly appeared before us, wearing very white clothes and with very black hair, without any signs of journey upon him, and none of us had seen him before. He sat before the holy prophet, with his knees touching the knees of the Messenger of Allah and he placed his hands on his thighs and said: O' Muhammad tell me about Islam. The Apostle of Allah said: 'Islam is to bear witness that none has the right to be worshipped but Allah and Muhammad is the Messenger of Allah, to offer the *Salat*, pay *Zakat*, Fast during the month of *Ramadhan* and to perform *Hajj* (pilgrimage to the holy Ka'ba in Makkah) if you are able and have the means to make the journey; That man said: 'you spoke the truth'. We were surprised at his asking and confirming at the same time. He said: 'Tell me about *Iman*' The Prophet said: '*Iman* is to believe in Allah, His angels, His Books and Messengers, the Last Day and to believe in the Divine pre-decree of all that is good and evil? He again said: 'you spoke the truth! And he said: Tell me about *Ihsan*'. He (the Apostle of Allah) said: '*Ihsan* (perfection) is to worship Allah as if you see Him; if you cannot see Him, surely He sees you? He said: Tell me about the (final) Hour. The Messenger of Allah remarked: The one asked has no more knowledge of it than the questioner: He said: 'Inform me about its signs! He (the Apostle of Allah) said: (its signs are) the slave girl will give birth to her mistress and you will see the bare footed, naked, impoverished sheepherders competing with each other in (constructing) tall buildings. Thereafter the stranger left and I

(Umar) remained sitting for quite a while: Then the prophet asked me: O Umar, do you know who that man was? I replied: Allah and His Messenger know best! He said: That was *Jibrael* (Gabriel) who had come to teach the people their religion.

For the conservation of a true religious spirit Islam emphasized certain practical duties, of which the following are principal — prayer, fasting alms giving and pilgrimage.

In instituting prayer Prophet Muhammad (peace & blessings of Allah be with him) recognized the yearning of the human soul to pour out its love and gratitude to Allah, and by making the devotion periodic, he impressed that disciplinary character of the observance of prayer that keeps the thoughts from wandering in to the regions of the material. The value of prayer as the means of moral elevation and the purification of the heart, has been clearly set forth in the Qur'an:

> "Rehearse that which has been revealed unto thee of the Book, and be constant in prayer, for prayer preserveth from crimes and from that which is blameworthy; and remembering of Allah is surely a most sacred duty."

It is one of the glories of Islam, says Hunter, that its temples are not made with hands, and that its ceremonies can be performed anywhere upon God's earth or under His heaven.

The religion of Islam recognizes no caste of priesthood, allows no monopoly of spiritual knowledge or special holiness to intervene between man and his Creator. Each soul rises to its Creator without the intervention of priests. Each human being is his own priest, and no man is higher than the other.

It is also made unmistakably clear by the Qur'an that piety of the believer is the most important thing in the sight of Allah.

> 'It is not righteousness, says the Qur'an, that ye turn your faces in prayer towards the east or west, but righteousness is of him who believeth in Allah who giveth money

for Allah's sake unto his kindered, and unto orphans, and the needy, and the stranger, and those who ask, and for the redemption of captives; who is constant at prayers and giveth alms; and of those who fulfill their covenant, when they have covenanted, and who are patient in hardship and adversity, and in times of violence. These are they who are true.'

It was emphasized that prayer without "the presence of the heart" was of no avail, and that Allah's words, which are addressed to all mankind and not to some people, should be performed with the heart and lips in absolute accord. And Hadrat Ali remarked that devotion offered without understanding was useless and brought no blessing.

Imam Ghazali opined that in reading the sacred Book heart and intelligence must work together. The lips only utter the words, intelligence helps in the due understanding of their meaning, the heart, in paying obedience to the dictates of duty. Only that devotion is acceptable to Allah that is offered with understanding and true devotional spirit. *(Reported by Abu Dawud from Muaz ibn Jabal).*

The Prophet (peace & blessings of Allah be with him) emphasized cleanliness as a necessary preliminary to the worship and adoration of Allah. At the same time, he cautioned that mere external, or rather physical, purity does not imply true devotion. He distinctly laid down that Almighty can only be approached in purity and humility of spirit. The holy Prophet (peace & blessings of Allah be with him) declared the most important purification to be the cleaning of the heart from all blameworthy inclinations and frailties, and the mind from all vicious ideas and from all thoughts that distract attention from Allah.

The institution of fasting has existed more or less among all communities, but it may be said that throughout the ancient world the idea attached to it was, without exception, more of penitence than of abstinence. The institution of fasting in Islam, on the contrary, seeks to restrain passions, by abstinence for a limited and definite period, from all the gratification of the senses. Fasting is prescribed to the able bodied and strong as a means of chastening the spirit by imposing a restraint on the body.

No religion before Islam had consecrated charity, the support of the widow, the orphan, and the helpless poor, by giving away a fixed portion every year from saved wealth.

General charity is inculcated in the Qur'an in most forcible terms:

> *Blessed are they who believe and humbly offer their thanksgiving to their Lord... who are constant in their charity, and who guard their chastity, and who observe their trust and covenants... Verily Allah bids you to do justice and good, and give to kindred their due; and He forbids you sin and to do wrong and oppress.*

Another pillar of Islam is the pilgrimage to the holy Kabah. Known as the *Hajj*. It is an exercise par excellence in devoting oneself to Allah, in overcoming one's egoism and in surrendering one's whole being to Allah. The *Hajj* is a supreme act of worship. It is a means for the believers to renew their faith in Allah. In spirit, *Hajj* combines all the other acts of worship. While other acts of worship are about remembering Allah; *Hajj* is about reaching Him. When pilgrims stand before the holy Ka'bah It is like standing before Allah. It is not the rites of worship that are so important during *Hajj* but the spirit in which they are carried out.

This is the Islam revealed to Prophet Muhammad (peace & blessings of Allah be with him). It is not a mere creed, it is a life to be lived in the present; a religion of right doing, right-thinking and right speaking, founded on divine love, universal charity, and the equality of humans in the sight of the Lord.

TAWHEED
(Monotheism)

TAWHEED
(Monotheism)

The concepts, attitudes, moral values and guidance of Islamic religion for human behaviour and relationships stem from affirmation of faith in *'La ilaha illa Allah, Muhammadur Rasul Allah'* (There is no deity except Allah, Muhammad is the Messenger of Allah or none is worthy of worship save Allah and Muhammad is the Messenger of Allah.) This simple statement of a Muslim's basic belief is the starting Point for all that follows.

The words *'La ilaha illa Allah'* attests not only to the oneness and uniqueness of Allah, it signifies, at the same time, the oneness of the lordship, the sovereignty and authority in the universe and this world. Allah, the Lord of all creation, Creates what He pleases, giving each of His creation the nature, function and role which He desires for it, in this He is accountable to no one and all things are under His absolute control.

The purpose for which He created human beings is to acknowledge, worship and obey Him alone, and at the same time to manage the affairs of this world and administer it with justice and righteousness according to His all-wise laws.

Islam teaches the purest form of Monotheism and regards

polytheism as the deadliest sin. Allah is the One God, Who is indivisible in person and Who has no partner. He is the Matchless and *"naught is His likeness"*. He is the First, the Last, the Eternal, the Infinite, the Almighty, the Omniscient, and the Omnipresent. He is the Creator, the Nourisher, and the Cherisher of all things. He is the All-Just, the Compassionate, the Merciful, the Loving, the Guide, the Friend, the Magnificent, the Glorious, the Beautiful and the True.

The Qur'an is a glorious testimony to the unity of God, writes Gibbon. The Prophet of Mecca rejected the worship of idols and men, of stars and planets, on the rational principle that whatever is corruptible must decay and perish, that whatever is born must die, that whatever rises must set.

From the Unity of the Creator proceeds the Unity of the Universe, that is, the unity of creation and unity of purpose. In other words, the Cosmos is a Moral Order. In the Islamic worldview therefore the whole of mankind is an "organic unity" and distinctions of race, colour, language, or territory are no basis for superiority of the one over the other. The only distinction that is valued is that which arises at the moral and spiritual planes, namely the distinction of *'taqwa'* or piety and righteousness.

Surah 112 of the holy Qur'an is a concise definition of Allah:

"Say: He is Allah, The One; Allah the Eternal, the Absolute; He begetteth not, nor is He begotten, and there is none like unto Him"

The exclusive submission to the Creator alone invests human beings with greatness and sublimity. Through this they are freed from obeying and serving anything less than Allah, the only Being who can ever be worthy of his devotion and obedience. *La-ilaha illallah* is therefore that powerful statement of faith, which represents the liberation of the one who professes it from a feeling of servitude and submission to anything or anyone other than Allah, Most High. It is the denial of all other claimants to divinity and supreme authority, the affirmation of Allah's oneness and sovereignty, and the statement of belief in and acceptance of His guidance as revealed to Prophet Muhammad (peace & blessings of Allah be with him), the last of Allah's Messengers.

Those who understand the significance of this concise formula of *Tawheed* and act according to its requirements are worthy of paradise.

'Whoever says *La ilaha illa Allah* sincerely will enter paradise'. The Messenger of Allah (peace & blessings of Allah be with him) is reported to have said. According to a *Hadith* recorded by Imam Muslim the Apostle of Allah said:

Whoever says *La ilaha illa Allah* and rejects whatever is worshipped besides Allah, his property and blood becomes sacred and his reckoning is (only) with Allah, the Mighty and Exalted.

The word *La ilaha illa Allah* will benefit the one who says it and conforms to its meaning in his life, and does not nullify it by associating partners with Allah. According to a *Hadith* reported by Baihaqi, the Messenger of Allah (peace & blessings of Allah be with him) said:

'Whoever says *La ilaha illa Allah*, it will be his salvation someday, no matter what befalls him before that.'

Of all the theological concepts, *Tawheed*, the Divine Unity, is the unifying idea that is inimical to tribalism, racism, casteism, and ethnocentricism. It opens up the horizon of universality and brotherhood of man. The basic call of *Tawheed* of no god but Allah, is essentially a call towards the unity of religions and unity of mankind.

And Muhammad is the Messenger of Allah

The second part of the *Shahada*, that is, '*Muhammadur Rasool Allah*' implies that Allah reveals His knowledge through his Messengers and Muhammad (peace & blessings of Allah be with him) is the last of the Prophets chosen by Allah to guide humanity on the right path.

For given the limited nature of human understanding the only possible means by which human beings can have access to certain knowledge is that Allah Himself reveals this knowledge by whatever means He deems fit. According to Islamic belief, since the dawn of human consciousness, the creator not only implanted in human beings the awareness of His existence, the innate knowledge that there is non-corporeal, transcendent Being Who created them and the world around them.

He also provided them with the answers to these vital questions that have occupied their minds, conveying His guidance to humanity through His messengers. Such messengers were raised in all regions and among all communities. However, overtime much of the message was subverted and lost. Nevertheless enough has survived of the ancient scriptures revealed to prophet Abraham, Moses, Jesus and others to make it clear that divine message has been one and the same: that there is a single, unique Being Who is the Lord and Master of all creation and that each individual is accountable to this Supreme Being for his or her deeds in this worldly life.

In this sense Islam does not claim to be a new religion; it is only the final religion that succeeds earlier religions. At the same time it is the original religion, that primordial faith which has had its roots deep in human consciousness since the first true human being walked upon the earth, the faith revealed to and preached by all the prophets: the religion of submission and accountability to the One Allah. Islam teaches the divine origin of this message, pointing to the similarity and continuity of the teachings brought by various messengers of Allah throughout human existence, but it makes it clear that during the course of time the divine message was subverted and distorted. Hence the divine origin of these messengers is to be believed in but not necessarily in their present form or content, since their present condition makes it impossible to determine what part of them has been changed either accidentally or deliberately, at the hands of men. All the true prophets of Allah are characterized by their total submission to Allah and their nearness to Him, their pure and upright nature, the extraordinary righteousness of their conduct, and their unswerving commitment to the mission with which they were entrusted.

The first concern of all the prophets in every age and in every environment was to correct the belief of the people regarding Allah, to correct the relationship between the servant and his Lord, to single out Allah as the only object of worship, and believing with all sincerity and certainty that He is the sole Dispenser of benefit and harm, the only One Who has the right to be worshipped and supplicated. Their mission focused against paganism, which was exemplified in the worship of idols, saints and humans, dead or alive.

However, Islam most emphatically denies any suggestion of divinity or super-human nature of the Messenger of Allah-Prophet Muhammad (peace & blessings of Allah be with him).

Allah addresses Prophet Muhammad through the holy Qur'an:

> Say (O Muhammad) I possess no power of benefit or hurt except as Allah wills. If I had the knowledge of the unseen (Ghayb), I should have secured for myself an abundance of wealth, and no evil should have touched me. I am but a Warner, and a bearer of glad tidings unto the people who believe. (Q. VII: 188).

In a *Hadith* recorded by Imam Bukhari, The holy Prophet (peace & blessings of Allah be with him) himself reportedly warned the faithful: Do not exaggerate in praising me as the Christians did to (Jesus) the son of Mary, for I am only a servant, so say (Muhammad is) the servant of Allah and His Messenger.

This warning implies that the Messenger of Allah is not

to be worshipped, not to be supplicated, as is the practice in other religions.

Again the holy Prophet (peace & blessings of Allah be with him) is reported by Tirmidhi to have remarked:

> *When you ask; ask from Allah. And when you seek help; seek the help of Allah.*

Allah alone is to be worshipped and prayed to. The holy Prophet (peace & blessings of Allah be with him) shall continue to be loved and praised by the believers across the world. However true love of the Prophet (peace & blessings of Allah be with him) lies in following his guidance in matters of religion, piety and other things.

Belief in the Unseen (*Ghayb*)

Although many people profess to believe in Allah, this is often a static belief, a mere opinion that Allah exists, which has no significant practical consequences and does not in an way affect the way they lead their lives.

Others do believe strongly in the supernatural but such belief is often vague, based on guesswork or unreliable knowledge about the ultimate reality of existence, especially of Allah as the center and source of the Reality.

Islam deals in a clear, straightforward manner with all such issues. There is a realm of existence, according to Islamic belief, which is beyond human perception known as *al-Ghayb*, that is the realm of the unseen. That which is known is termed as *ash-shahadah* — the evident or witnessed.

In Islam belief in the unseen realm is a prerequisite for belief in and understanding of that part of creation which are beyond human senses and faculties but which is, nonetheless, of fundamental importance to his existence.

According to the Islamic belief what is visible and perceptible to human faculties — *ash shahadah* — is only a small part of the totality of what exists and which only its Creator knows.

However, even though the wider Reality cannot be perceived directly, there are many evidences that are known to us. Among these is the physical universe itself, which is eloquent testimony of the might, wisdom and creativity of Allah. The human being is another striking evidence.

In Islam Allah is the center of total Reality. Indeed, He is the Reality. Allah is the Creator, Sustainer, and Nourisher of all that exists. He is the Alternator of night and day He is the Supreme, the All-knowing and the All-wise, the Merciful, the Gracious, the Loving and the Forgiving. And Allah is alone in the heavens (Fis sama). In the holy Qur'an Allah proclaims:

> 'Do you feel secure that He, Who is over the heaven will not cause the earth to sink with you' (Q. 67: 16).

The belief that Allah is above the heavens is considered as an indicator of the soundness of one's belief and is considered mandatory on every believer. This is to refute the erroneous belief that Allah is in every place by His self. The truth is that Allah is with us by His knowledge not by His self.

In the holy book Allah proclaims:

> "Say (O Muhammad) ' He is Allah, the One, the Self – Sufficient. He begets not, nor is He begotten, and there is none like Him (Q. 112: 1-4).

And Again:

> Whatever is in the heavens and on the earth glorifies Allah, for He is the Mighty, the Wise. To Him belongs the dominion of the heavens and the earth. It is He who gives life and death, and He has power over all things. He is the First and the Last, the Evident, and the Immanent, and He has full knowledge of all things. (Q. 27: 1-3).

And:

> There is no deity except Allah. He knows the unseen (al-Ghayb) and the Evident (Ash-Shahadah) He is the Merciful... To Him belong the most beautiful names.

Whatever is in the heavens and the earth glorifies Him, and He is the Mighty, the Wise (Q. 59: 22-24).

Allah is thus the Originator and Designer of the universe with all its vast and perfect systems, the One who sustains and keeps it functioning according to His infinitely wise plans and laws. And certainly and clearly He is beyond anything that human mind or senses may grasp or comprehend or imagine or explain, and that He is far, far above having any similarity to any of His creations.

Yet as the ultimate Reality, Allah has absolute relevance and meaning for every single human being since it is solely in relation to Allah that we exist and move through the journey of this life on our way back to Him.

According to the Islamic belief Allah is creatively involved with every single part of His creation with every part of its macro and micro systems. For His interest is not merely in creating but also in sustaining, nourishing, directing and guiding.

Amongst the creatures of this universe man is a unique creation of Allah. Humans possess an obvious, outward aspect — the physical body — and a hidden inner aspect — the mind, emotions and soul. The unique status of man lies in that he has been endowed with freedom of choice and judgment between right and wrong, capacities for thinking, feeling and expressing, and an immortal soul that lives on after the death of the physical body.

Allah crated humans with complex and multi-faceted nature in order that they may form a smoothly functioning, harmonious whole. This in itself constitutes the great task, the ultimate challenge, of being human. Each element of man's nature has its role and function. Its legitimate needs and right to satisfaction; but in order to bring about harmony which Allah intends, among them, the individual is required to exercise his will and govern them according to the laws which Allah has laid down for his well-being, thus achieving synthesis, integration and balance within his personality. This is why Islam concerns itself not merely with religious and spiritual matters but with all aspects of human life, all of which falls within the framework of religion in the Islamic sense of the term, treating man as an indivisible, organic whole in keeping with the reality of his uniquely human nature.

Allah expects believers to use their freedom of choice to voluntarily choose what Allah wants for them rather than to follow their own random and often chaotic desires; that is, to submit their will to Allah's higher will and by this means to carry out the responsibilities, both personal and collective, which Allah has entrusted to them. For Allah alone possesses the all-embracing, absolute knowledge and wisdom to provide His creatures with guidance that will lead to their assured well-being in this world and in the Hereafter.

A conscientious Muslim believes that he is nothing but a humble slave before his Lord. It follows that there must be no other lords and authorities in his life besides Allah. Islam proclaims that all other elements that claim obedience and devotion of humans, and which attempt to rule or dominate his life are false.

Freedom of choice for humans, in the Islamic belief, is between two possible ways:

- To be in bondage to human ideas and notions and desires, or to consciously and voluntarily commit oneself to be bound by the standards, criteria and laws of Allah alone.
- To be slave of human masters, living by man-made values, philosophies and doctrines, or to be the slave of the true Master of men, Allah, the Most High.

True freedom does not consist of license to do whatever one wants while being the slave of one's own particular deity, rather freedom consists of being free from enslavement to anything or anyone other than one's real Master. Islam's unique task is thus to liberate man from enslavement and servitude to anything other than Allah, and to free him to worship and serve Him alone.

A Muslim is expected to believe that all that is good and bad exists by Allah's Decree, knowledge and Will. But, at the same time, every individual is responsible for his or her good or evil actions. The observation of Allah's commands and prohibitions are mandatory upon the believers and it is not lawful to disobey Allah and then consider it Allah's decree. Allah raised His prophets and revealed to them His Books to show the path of happiness and misery, and blessed humans with the faculty and ability to think. He made known to humankind the difference between guidance and error.

Thus proclaims Allah in the Holy Book:

Verily, we showed him the way, whether he be grateful or ungrateful (Q. 76: 3).

Therefore, through his or her actions an individual may strengthen, weaken or nullify faith (*Iman*) and religion.

Belief in materialist or atheist philosophies nullifies faith. Marxists and materialists deny the existence of God and believe that the world and life therein is purely a material phenomenon, a product of nature or chance. Muslims Must remember, however, what Allah proclaims in the holy Book:

Allah is the Creator of all things, and He is the Wakil (Trustee / Guardian etc.) *over all things (Q. 39: 62)*

Throughout history some powerful men have claimed that they are god or god – incarnate. For instance the Pharaoh said: I am your lord, most high *(Q. 79: 24).*

It is also believed by some Muslims that some great saints have control over what happens in the universe and some Sufis preached that Allah pervades in His creation. Such views are nothing but heresy.

A believer must remember that polytheism (*shirk*) nullifies *iman*. Ascribing partners to Allah is a great sin. The life history of prophet Muhammad (peace & blessings of Allah be with him) was a struggle against this sin. He taught us that neither the stars, the sun and the moon, nor man made idols, not even the dead saints have any power to do good or harm. Allah brands such people as *Kafirun* (disbelievers):

> "And those whom you invoke or call upon instead of Him, own not even a Qitmir (the thin membrane over the date seed). If you invoke them they hear not your call, and if (in case) they were to hear, they could not grant it (your request) to you. And on the Day of Reckoning, they will disown your worshipping them. And none can inform you (O' Muhammad) like Him who is the All-Knower (Q. 35: 13-14)

The holy Book is explicit that whoever worships and supplicates others than Allah, is a *Mushrik* (polytheist) even if he believes that those other things can neither benefit nor harm, but only sees them as intercessors.

Among the nullifiers of faith is to rule or judge by other than what Allah has revealed if it is accompanied by the belief that the laws of Allah are inappropriate or less appropriate, or that man made laws which contradict them are equally appropriate.

> Allah, the Most High, says: *And whosoever does not judge by what Allah has revealed, such are the Kafirun (disbelievers) (Q. 5: 44).*

The holy prophet (peace & blessings of Allah be with him) is reported to have said (as reported by ibn Abbas) that 'whoever repudiates what Allah has revealed, then he surely disbelieved, while one who accepted it, he is unjust and corrupt.' Faith is also nullified when names of Allah or His attributes established by the text of the Qur'an and the authentic *Sunnah* are denied. It is an error to interpret the affirmed Attributes of Allah and to change the meaning of the words used to describe Him from their primary meaning in the Arabic language to obscure meanings. There are certain Attributes that are exclusive to Allah, like knowledge of the Unseen (*Ghayb*), which no one among His creation possess. Allah proclaims in the Qur'an: *'And with Him are the keys of the Ghayb* (all that is hidden) *none knows them but He..."* (Q. 6:59).

However Allah may reveal certain aspects of the unseen to His messengers through revelation when He wills. Thus the holy Book says: (He alone) *the All-knower of the Ghayb* (unseen), *and He reveals to none His Ghayb except to a Messenger whom He has chosen* (Q.72: 26).

Likewise rejecting any of the prophets of Allah and defaming them nullifies faith. It is a sin to disparage the Messenger of Allah (peace & blessings of Allah be with him) or his truthfulness or sincerity or his chasteness or to revile him or poke fun at him, or to find fault with his behaviour.

It is grave error to attack authentic *Ahadith* or to disbelieve them, to deny any of the stories and sayings with regard to the prophets of Allah as reported in the Qur'an or narrated by the Apostle of Allah (peace & blessings of Allah be with him).

And whoever denies the finality of prophethood of Muhammad (peace & blessings of Allah be with him) commits the gravest sin and has forfeited his or her right to be a Muslim. As Allah proclaims in the holy Book:

> *Muhammad is the Messenger of Allah, and the last of the Prophets* (Q. 33:40).

At the same time to describe the Prophet (peace & blessings of Allah be with him) with attributes which belong to Allah alone such as the knowledge of the unseen or to pray to the Prophet tantamounts to *shirk* and contradicts the preaching and status of the Prophet. The holy Book proclaims:

> *'And there is no victory except by the help of Allah'* (Q.8:10).

Divine Pre-decree

To believe in Divine pre-decree is one of the fundamentals of the Islamic faith. According to Imam An-Nawawi 'Verily Allah decreed all matters before their existence, and Allah knows exactly when and where every thing will occur, and everything occurs according to His Decree. The holy Book Proclaims:

> *No misfortune can befall on earth or in you but is recorded in a Book* (of Allah's Decrees) *before Allah brings it into existence (Q. 57: 22)*

Belief in Allah's Decree is the final article of faith in Islam. Since the entire scheme and plan of creation is under the direction and control of the Almighty Creator and Sustainer, every thing that is, or that happens in the universe, from the smallest to the greatest events, is governed by Allah's will. It is an integral part of His eternal plan. Nothing can take place without His ordaining it, nor is there such a thing as a random, chance event.

Allah says in the holy Book:

> *No calamity befalls, but with the leave of Allah (Q. 64: 11)*

According to Ibn Abbas: His leave or permission means, His command and decree.

The true Muslim lives with the clear certainty that Allah is absolutely Real and that He is continuously active in all of His creation. All that exists or happens, therefore, is the expression of His will, from the behaviour of each atom of matter to the large-scale occurrences of human history to events of cosmic proportions. And since all of it is His, determined by His permission and decree, nothing that happens can ever be understood as 'intervention' or 'supernatural', or as a random, chance event devoid of meaning and purpose, whether it happens in the world of nature or in the world of humans. In human life, ease and suffering alike, and the events which produce them, equally have a purpose and meaning, and are equally a part of Allah's infinitely wise plan for His creation.

Such a belief gives the Muslim a great degree of inner certainty, confidence and peace of heart, especially in the face of afflictions, for he knows that since everything is under the control of the All-wise, Most-Merciful Allah, the circumstances of his life are likewise under His control and direction, and hence are not without a reason or purpose. And that nothing that Allah has not decreed for him can be brought about by any other means whatever.

This inner certainty frees the Muslim from fear of anyone or anything other than Allah, for he knows that no one has the slightest power either to injure or to benefit him without His leave.

Belief in Divine Decree leads to contentment, firmness in faith and the hope of divine rewards. Allah Almighty says in His Book: 'And whosoever believes in Allah, He guides his heart.' (Q. 64: 11).

According to Ibn Kathir this implies that when a person who is beset by misfortune and knows that it occurred by the order by Decree of Allah, remains patient, seeking thereby reward, in submission to Allah's Decree, Allah guides his heart, and compensates him for his material loss. According to Ibn Abbas, Allah guides his heart to conviction in faith, he knows what occurred to him was unavoidable, and what did not occur, could not have happened.

The holy prophet (peace & blessings of Allah be with him) is reported to have said: A Muslim is not beset by any hardship or fatigue or illness or grief or even a worry that Allah will not expiate thereby his sins. (*Sahih Muslim*).

According to another *Hadith* reported by Imam Ahmad the holy prophet (peace & blessings of Allah be with him) is reported to have said:

'Be satisfied with what Allah has apportioned for you, and you will be wealthiest of people'. And

'To be well off is not through possessing lots of transitory goods; rather well-being comes from a contented heart.'

For the patient and believing souls Allah has promised great rewards:

> "And give glad tidings to the patient ones who, when afflicted with calamity, say: Truly! To Allah we belong and truly, to Him we shall return! They are those on whom are the salawat (blessings etc.) from their Lord, and (they) receive His Mercy, and it is they who are the guided ones." (Q. 2: 155-157).

However, in any situation, Islam teaches that the task of human beings is to make a sincere effort, to strive, to do their best — not to sit back and let things take their course in blind resignation to some supposed 'fate' or 'destiny'. For a human being does not know and cannot know wherein his destiny lies, and until he has exhausted all possible means and what inevitably occurs, he cannot be said to have encountered that destiny. But then whatever Allah decides, whatever befalls one, after all his efforts have been made, should be accepted with patience and gratitude towards the Lord.

Belief in Divine decree is thus a statement of faith in the meaningfulness and purposefulness of all that is, and essential part of the Muslim's sense of total trust, dependence and submission to Allah.

The holy prophet (peace & blessings of Allah be with him) is reported to have said: The strong believer is better and more beloved to Allah than the weak believer, though both are good; work hard for that which is beneficial to you and seek the help of Allah and do not give up (*Bukhari*).

SALAT
(Prayer)

SALAT
(Prayer)

"Establish regular prayer; for prayer restraints from shameful and unjust deeds; and remembrance of Allah is the greatest (thing in life) without' doubt. And Allah knoweth (the deeds) that ye do." (Q. 29:45).

The first obligation of a Muslim is to establish the Islamic worship on a regular basis. This implies to observe *Salat* regularly five times a day at proper times, as well as the obligatory congregational Friday Prayer.

Salat is the central point of the existence of a Muslim.

Thus no matter where on earth he may be, it is at once his duty and a necessity of his being to maintain *salat*, faithfully and whenever possible in the company of his fellow-Muslims. Praying inside a mosque is praiseworthy but as the holy prophet (peace & blessings of Allah be with him) said:

The whole world is my mosque.

Basically *Salat* consists of recitation from the Qur'an and glorification of Allah accompanied by various bodily postures.

The five times of worship correspond to five periods of the day: daybreak, noon, afternoon, sunset, and night.

Salat can be performed almost anywhere — in a mosque, at home, place of work, outdoors or either individually or collectively. Congregational *Salat* is considered praiseworthy, especially for offering the *Fard* (obligatory) prayers.

So great is the importance of *Salat* that it is an obligation under all circumstances — during illness, travel or in battle. However, certain concessions are permitted in some situations. Thus, one who is ill and cannot perform *Salat* in the usual manner may pray sitting in a chair or lying in bed. If a *Salat* is missed, it is to be made up as soon as possible thereafter. The sole exception to this are the women who are exempted during menstruation and up to forty days, following child birth.

Salat is a multifaceted act of worship. Performing it regularly serves as a repeated reminder to the Muslims during the day and night of his relationship with his Creator and his place in the total scheme of Reality. The purpose of *Salat* is to remind a believer that he or she belongs to Allah and that he or she is His slave, obedient to His command. The remembrance of the Lord and glorification of Him for a brief, concentrated period, in the midst of daily activities, keeps this perspective always clear and intact. No matter how faithful or conscientious an individual may be such reminders are essential, for human involvement in worldly concerns and activities is so engrossing that one can easily forget the Lord.

While the purpose of prayer or worship is the remembrance and glorification of Allah Most High, a believer must remember that Allah's Majesty and Glory do not depend in the slightest degree upon the praise or even acknowledgement by His creatures, for He is absolutely independent of His creation and free of all needs; rather the humans need to worship Him to keep their contact with their Lord and their own vision of Reality clear and strong.

The purpose of prayer, therefore, is to strengthen the individual's faith and sense of submission to Allah, to fortify his character, to discipline himself as Allah's faithful servants on the earth.

Prayer is religion in action and through it a spirit establishes between itself and its Creator a relation of devotion and to whose will it submits. Prayer is not mere utterance of words or a repetition of certain phrases. It is a vital activity that the spirit performs to put itself in a private devotion of, and direct contact with the Lord. Communication between the human spirit and its Creator, even for a short time in a day, is a basic necessity to man.

Islamic *Salat* is truly the complete expression of man's voluntary submission to Allah, Most High. In addition, through the bodily postures of the prayer, which consists of standing, bowing, prostrating and sitting, repeated at specified number of times in each prayer, the Muslim expresses submission, humility and adoration of Allah with his entire being.

Indeed, the self-discipline that is needed to perform *Salat* regularly and at proper times reaffirms the total dependence of the servant on his Creator and his position as His slave. *Salat* is truly the complete expression of man's voluntary submission to Him. It is to be performed with strict concentration, attention and presence of the heart, not simply as a mechanical, verbal and physical exercise.

THE *ADHAN* (Call to Prayer) AND *IQAMAH* (Call to Begin The Prayer)

The *Adhan* is a distinctive feature of Islamic religious practice. It is the announcement that the time of a particular *Salat* has begun. This is done with a specific wording, and for the purpose of calling the people to pray in congregation.

The wordings of the *Adhan* are as follows:

اَذَانٌ

اَللّٰهُ اَكْبَرُ اَللّٰهُ اَكْبَرُ اَللّٰهُ اَكْبَرُ اَللّٰهُ اَكْبَرُ

Allahu Akbar, Allahu Akbar; Allahu Akbar, Allahu Akbar "
Allah is the Greatest. (repeated 4 times).

اَشْهَدُ اَنْ لَّا اِلٰهَ اِلَّا اللّٰهُ   اَشْهَدُ اَنْ لَّا اِلٰهَ اِلَّا اللّٰهُ

Ash-hadu an la Illaha illa Allah, Ash-hadu an La ilaha illa Allah "
I bear witness that none has the right to be worshipped save Allah." (twice)

اَشْهَدُ اَنَّ مُحَمَّدًا رَسُوْلُ اللّٰهِ   اَشْهَدُ اَنَّ مُحَمَّدًا رَسُوْلُ اللّٰهِ

Ash-hadu anna Muhammadan Rasul-ullah, Ash-hadu anna Muhammadan Rasul-ullah

"I bear witness that Muhammad is the Messenger of Allah." (twice)

حَيَّ عَلَى الصَّلٰوةِ   حَيَّ عَلَى الصَّلٰوةِ

Hayya 'alus-Salah, Hayya 'alas-Salah "
"Hurry towards *Salat*." (twice)

حَيَّ عَلَى الْفَلَاحِ   حَيَّ عَلَى الْفَلَاحِ

Hayya 'alal-Falah, Hayya 'alal-Falah "
"Hurry towards righteousness." (twice)

اَللّٰهُ اَكْبَرُ اَللّٰهُ اَكْبَرُ

Allahu Akbar, Allahu Akbar
"Allah is the Greatest." (twice)

لَا إِلَٰهَ إِلَّا اللَّهُ

La ilaha illa Allah

None has the right to be worshipped save Allah." (once)

In the call to prayer for *Fajr* (the Dawn Prayer) the *Mu'adh-dhin* (caller) adds after *Hayya 'alal-Falah*:

اَلصَّلٰوةُ خَيْرٌ مِّنَ النَّوْمِ ۔ اَلصَّلٰوةُ خَيْرٌ مِّنَ النَّوْمِ ۔

As-Salatu Khairum minan nawm, As-Salatu Khairum minan nawm

"The *Salat* is better than sleep." (twice)

إِقَامَةٌ

The *Iqamah*

Iqamah is like the *Adhan* but it is pronounced immediately before the start of obligatory prayer, in order to assemble the people in the mosque in orderly rows. The wordings of the *Iqamah* are as under:

اَللَّهُ اَكْبَرُ اَللَّهُ اَكْبَرُ

Allahu Akbar, Allahu Akbar

"Allah is the Greatest." (twice)

اَشْهَدُ اَنْ لَّا إِلٰهَ إِلَّا اللَّهُ

Ash-hadu an la ilaha illa Allah

"I bear witness that none has the right to be worshipped save Allah." (once)

اَشْهَدُ اَنَّ مُحَمَّدًا رَسُوْلُ اللَّهِ

Ash-hadu anna Muhammadan Rasul-ullah

"I bear witness that Muhammad is the Messenger of Allah." (once)

حَيَّ عَلَى الصَّلٰوةِ

Hayya 'alas-Salah

"Hurry towards *Salat*." (once)

حَيَّ عَلَى الْفَلَاحِ

Hayya 'alal-Falah

"Hurry towards righteousness." (once)

قَدْ قَامَتِ الصَّلٰوةُ قَدْ قَامَتِ الصَّلٰوةُ

Qad qamatis-Salah, Qad qamatis-Salah

"The *Salat* is being established." (twice)

اَللّٰهُ اَكْبَرُ اَللّٰهُ اَكْبَرُ

Allahu Akbar, Allahu Akbar

"Allah is the Greatest." (twice)

لَآ اِلٰهَ اِلَّا اللّٰهُ

La ilaha illa Allah

"None has the right to be worshipped save Allah." (once)

It is praiseworthy for one who hears the *Adhan* to repeat each phrase after the *Mu'adhdhin*, except when he says: "Hurry to *Salat*" and "Hurry to success," one should say:

لَاحَوْلَ وَلَا قُوَّةَ اِلَّا بِاللّٰهِ

La hawla wa la quwwata illa billah

"There is no power nor might except by Allah."

After the *Adhan* one should ideally seek blessings of Allah on the holy Prophet (peace & blessings of Allah be with him) in a low voice, then he should make the following supplication:

اَللّٰهُمَّ رَبَّ هٰذِهِ الدَّعْوَةِ التَّامَّةِ وَالصَّلوٰةِ الْقَائِمَةِ اٰتِ مُحَمَّدَ نِالْوَسِيْلَةَ وَالْفَضِيْلَةَ وَالدَّرَجَةَ الرَّفِيْعَةَ وَابْعَثْهُ مَقَامًا مَّحْمُوْدَ نِالَّذِيْ وَعَدْتَّهُ وَارْزُقْنَا شَفَاعَتَهُ يَوْمَ الْقِيَامَةِ اِنَّكَ لَا تُخْلِفُ الْمِيْعَادَ ۰

Allahumma rabba hadhi-hid da 'wa tit-tam-mati wa-sala til qa'imati ati Muhammada nil-waseelata wal fadeelata wab 'ath-hu maqamam mahmooda nil-ladhee wa 'ad tahu.

"O Allah, the Lord of this perfect call and established *Salat*, grant Muhammad intercession (in Your Court) and honour, and raise him to the position of praise on the Day of Judgment, which You promised him."

The holy Prophet (peace & blessings of Allah be with him) said:

Whoever supplicates with this *Du 'a'* after hearing the *Adhan* will be eligible for my intercession on the Day of Judgment. *(Bukhari)*

The *Adhan* is an act of worship, and worship should be performed in accordance with the teachings of the Prophet without addition or omission.

THE SALAT UL FAJR
(The Dawn Prayer)

- Make the intention to pray two *Rak 'ahs* (units) of *Fajr* (Dawn) *Salat* in your hearts and mind without saying it with the tongue.

- Face the *Qiblah* (the direction of the *Ka 'bah* in Makkah) raise your hands up to your ears and say:

"Allah is the Greatest"'

- Place your right hand on the back of your left hand on your chest and recite:

$$\text{سُبْحَانَكَ اللّٰهُمَّ وَبِحَمْدِكَ وَتَبَارَكَ اسْمُكَ وَتَعَالٰى جَدُّكَ وَلَآ اِلٰهَ غَيْرُكَ}$$

"Glory to you O Allah, and with Your Praise, and Your Name is Blessed and none has the right to be worshipped save You."

(one may recite any other *Du'a'*).

The First *Rak'ah*

Recite in a low tone:

$$\text{اَعُوْذُ بِاللّٰهِ مِنَ الشَّيْطَانِ الرَّجِيْمِ}$$

"I seek refuge with Allah from the accursed Satan.

$$\text{بِسْمِ اللّٰهِ الرَّحْمٰنِ الرَّحِيْمِ}$$

In the Name of Allah, the Most Gracious, the Most Merciful."

Recite the opening chapter of the Qur'an *(Al-Fatihah)*:

$$\text{اَلْحَمْدُ لِلّٰهِ رَبِّ الْعٰلَمِيْنَ ۙ اَلرَّحْمٰنِ الرَّحِيْمِ ۙ مَالِكِ يَوْمِ الدِّيْنِ ۙ اِيَّاكَ نَعْبُدُ وَاِيَّاكَ نَسْتَعِيْنُ ۙ اِهْدِنَا الصِّرَاطَ الْمُسْتَقِيْمَ ۙ صِرَاطَ الَّذِيْنَ اَنْعَمْتَ عَلَيْهِمْ ۙ غَيْرِ الْمَغْضُوْبِ عَلَيْهِمْ وَلَا الضَّآلِّيْنَ (آمين)}$$

"All the praises and thanks are due to Allah, the Lord of the Worlds (humankind, Jinns and all that exists). The Most Gracious, the Most Merciful. The Only Owner (and the Only Ruling Judge) of the Day of Resurrection. You (Alone) we worship, and You (Alone) we ask for help (for each and everything). Guide us to the Straight Path. The Path of those You have favoured, not (the path) of those who earned Your wrath, nor of those who went astray *(Q.1:1-7).*

Thereafter recite: *Ameen*

Recite:

$$\text{بِسْمِ اللّٰهِ الرَّحْمٰنِ الرَّحِيْمِ}$$

"In the Name of Allah, the Most Gracious, the Most Merciful."

Recite:

$$\text{قُلْ هُوَ اللّٰهُ اَحَدٌ ۚ اَللّٰهُ الصَّمَدُ ۚ لَمْ يَلِدْ ۙ وَلَمْ يُوْلَدْ ۙ وَلَمْ يَكُنْ لَّهُ كُفُوًا اَحَدٌ}$$

"Say: He is Allah, (the) One. The Self-Sufficient Master, Whom all creatures need, He neither eats nor drinks. He begets not, nor was He begotten. And there is none co-equal or comparable unto Him." *(Q.112:1-4)*

(Any Other *Surah* (chapter) or even a long verse of the Qur'an can also be recited, depending upon whatever is easy to remember.)

- Raise your hands and recite: "Allah is the Greatest," اَللّٰهُ اَكْبَرُ bow at the waist with your legs straight, grasping your knees, your back should be level. Recite three times in this position:

$$\text{سُبْحَانَ رَبِّيَ الْعَظِيْمِ}$$

Glory to my Lord, the Exalted.

- Raise your head and hands until you are standing straight. Recite, as you move:

$$\text{سَمِعَ اللّٰهُ لِمَنْ حَمِدَهُ}$$

"Allah hears those who praise Him",

and when you stand upright, say:

رَبَّنَا لَكَ الْحَمْدُ

"O Lord, all Praise is to You."

- Reciting "اَللّٰهُ اَكْبَرُ Allah is the Greatest" go down on your hands and knees and place your forehead and nose on the ground. Your toes should also be on the ground, pointing toward the *Qiblah,* your elbows should be off the ground and away from your sides. Recite three times:

سُبْحَانَ رَبِّيَ الْأَعْلَى

"Glory to my Lord, the Most High."

- Raise your head up, saying, اَللّٰهُ اَكْبَرُ "Allah is the Greatest", until you come to a sitting position with your legs folded beneath you. Place your palms on your thighs with the fingers ending at the beginning of the knees and say:

رَبِّ اغْفِرْلِيْ وَارْحَمْنِيْ وَاهْدِنِيْ وَعَافِنِيْ وَارْزُقْنِيْ

"O Lord, forgive me, have mercy on me, guide me, protect me and provide me with sustenance."

- Prostrate on the ground a second time, saying: اَللّٰهُ اَكْبَرُ "Allah is the Greatest" as you move, and recite three times:

سُبْحَانَ رَبِّيَ الْأَعْلَى

"Glory to my Lord, the Most High."

- Raise your head a second time, saying " اَللّٰهُ اَكْبَرُ Allah is the Greatest" sit briefly as before, resting your bottoms on the sole of your left foot, with the right foot propped up, the toes touching the ground and pointing towards the *Qiblah.*

The Second *Rak'ah*

- Rise up to a standing position with your hands placed (right over left on the chest) as before. Recite:

$$اَعُوْذُ بِاللّٰهِ مِنَ الشَّيْطَانِ الرَّجِيْمِ۔$$

I seek refuge with Allah from accursed Satan, and say:

$$بِسْمِ اللّٰهِ الرَّحْمٰنِ الرَّحِيْمِ۔$$

"In the Name of Allah, the Most Gracious, the Most Merciful",

Thereafter recite *Surah Fatihah* and any other *Surah* or whatever is easy for you from the Qur'an.

- Make *Ruku'* (bowing) and two *Sajdah* (prostration) as in the first *Rak'ah*. After rising from the second *Sajdah*, sit like before with your right foot propped up, close the fingers of the right hand, and extend the index finger, raise it and recite (*At-Tahiyyah*):

$$اَلتَّحِيَّاتُ لِلّٰهِ وَالصَّلَوٰتُ وَالطَّيِّبَاتُ اَلسَّلَامُ عَلَيْكَ اَيُّهَا النَّبِيُّ وَرَحْمَةُ اللّٰهِ وَبَرَكَاتُهُ۔ اَلسَّلَامُ عَلَيْنَا وَعَلٰى عِبَادِ اللّٰهِ الصّٰلِحِيْنَ۔ اَشْهَدُ اَنْ لَّا اِلٰهَ اِلَّا اللّٰهُ وَاَشْهَدُ اَنَّ مُحَمَّدًا عَبْدُهُ وَرَسُوْلُهُ۔$$

"All the greetings of humility, prayers and good things are due to Allah; peace be on you, O Prophet, and Allah's Mercy and Blessings be on you. Peace be on us and on the pious worship-pers of Allah. I testify that none has the right to be worshiped but Allah and I also testify that Muhammad is His slave and His Messenger."

Thereafter recite *Darud*:

$$اَللّٰهُمَّ صَلِّ عَلٰى مُحَمَّدٍ وَّعَلٰى اٰلِ مُحَمَّدٍ كَمَا صَلَّيْتَ عَلٰى اِبْرَاهِيْمَ وَعَلٰى اٰلِ اِبْرَاهِيْمَ اِنَّكَ حَمِيْدٌ مَّجِيْدٌ۔$$

اَللّٰهُمَّ بَارِكْ عَلٰى مُحَمَّدٍ وَّعَلٰى اٰلِ مُحَمَّدٍ كَمَا بَارَكْتَ عَلٰى اِبْرَاهِيْمَ وَعَلٰى اٰلِ اِبْرَاهِيْمَ اِنَّكَ حَمِيْدٌ مَّجِيْدٌ

O Allah! Send Your *Salat* (Blessings Graces, Honors and Mercy) on Muhammad and the family of Muhammad as You sent Your *Salat* on Ibrahim and the family of Ibrahim. Oh Allah! Send Your Blessings on Muhammad and the family of Muhammad as You sent Your Blessings on Ibrahim and the family of Ibrahim. You are praiseworthy, Most Gracious."

Then recite:

اَللّٰهُمَّ اِنِّىْ اَعُوْذُبِكَ مِنْ عَذَابِ جَهَنَّمَ وَمِنْ عَذَابِ الْقَبْرِ وَمِنْ فِتْنَةِ الْمَحْيَا وَالْمَمَاتِ وَمِنْ فِتْنَةِ الْمَسِيْحِ الدَّجَّالِ

"O Allah, I seek refuge with You from the torment of Hell, and from the torment of the grave, and from the trial of life and death and from the trial of the *Dajjal* (the Antichrist)."

- Then turn your head to the right (looking over the right shoulder), saying:

اَلسَّلَامُ عَلَيْكُمْ وَرَحْمَةُ اللّٰهِ

"Peace be upon you and the Mercy of Allah." Then turn your head to the left (looking over the left shoulder) and say the same.

- After *Salat* there are certain supplications of Allah's remembrance, which are recommended in the *Sunnah*. For instance: *Ayat-ul-Kursi* (the Verse of the Kursi - 2:255); the last three *Surahs* of the Qur'an; *Subhan Allah, Al-Hamdulillah,* and *Allahu Akbar*-33 times each; and other supplications like:

اَللّٰهُمَّ اَعِنِّىْ عَلٰى ذِكْرِكَ وَشُكْرِكَ وَحُسْنِ عِبَادَتِكَ

"O Allah help me to remember You and express gratitude to You and to worship You in the best way."

As well as other supplications.

THE BASICS OF SALAT

- *Salat* is mandatory on every sane, adult Muslim. The Prophet (peace & blessings of Allah be with him) said:

"The pen is lifted from three persons (i.e. they will not be taken to account): the insane whose rationality has been eroded until he recovers, the sleeper until he wakes, and the children until they attain puberty." *(Abu Dawud)*

The Prophet (peace & blessings of Allah be with him) said:

"Teach your children *Salat* when they reach seven, and spank them for (neglecting) it when they reach ten." *(Ahmad)*. There are certain *Salat* that are highly recommended. Some of them are prayed Just before and some Just after the obligatory *Salat*. The holy Prophet (peace & blessings of Allah be with him), who used to offer them regularly, recommended them.

- Do not rush through your prayers, fix your gaze upon your place of prostration and do not look around or close you eyes.

- If the *Imam* recites out loud, be quiet and listen; if the *Imam* recites to himself, recite in a low voice so that you can hear yourself but others do not (except Al-Fatihah which should be recited in both cases in a low voice).

- The Dawn prayer consists of two *Sunnah Rakahs* before *Fard*, and Two *Rakah Fard*. The *Dhuhr* prayer consists of Two plus two *Sunnah Rakahs* plus Four *Fard* plus two *Sunnah*. The *Asr* prayer consists of two plus two *Sunnah* and Four *Fard*. The *Maghreb* prayer consists of Two *Sunnah*, three *Fard* and two *Sunnah*. *Isha'* prayer comprises of two *Sunnah*, four *Fard* and two plus three *Sunnah* or one *Witr Rakahs*.

- The obligatory *Salat* of *Jumu'ah* has two *Rak'ahs* which cannot be offered anywhere but in the mosque after the *Khutbah* (sermon).

- The obligatory *Salat* of *Maghrib* is three *Rak'ahs*; the first two *Rak'ahs* are like *Fajr* but after sitting in the second *Rak'ah* and reciting the *Tahiyyat*. Recite upto "I bear witness that Muhammad is His slave and Messenger," do not recite anything further and do not make *Taslim*. (salutation), but say: *Allahu Akbar* and stand up raising your hands to the shoulders. Then recite *Surah Fatihah* only and thereafter the rest of the *Rak'ah* is the same as the second. Finish the *Salat* by making *Taslim* to the right and then the left.

- The obligatory *Salat* of *Dhuhr*, *Asr*, and *'Isha'* comprises of four *Rak'ahs* each. The first two *Rak'ahs* are Just like *Fajr*, but when sitting in the second *Rak'ah* after reciting the *Tahiyyat*, do not make *Taslim*, but stand for the third *Rak'ah*, and then for the fourth, reciting *Surah Fatihah* only in the last two Rakahs. When you finish, make *Taslim* to the right and the left.

- *Witr* is three *Rak'ahs*. Pray two *Rak'ahs* and end with *Taslim* to right and the left. Then pray a single *Rak'ah* by itself, and it is best to supplicate with the following *Masnûn Du'a'* before going into *Ruku'* by lifting the hands and saying:

"O Allah guide along with those whom You have guided, and grant me well-being along with those whom You have granted well-being, and take care of me along with those whom You have taken care of, and bless me in what You have bestowed, and protect me from the evil of what You have decreed, for verily You decree and none can impose a decree upon You, and whomsoever You took as a friend will never be disgraced. And whomsoever You took as an enemy will not be honoured. You are blessed, our Lord, High and Exalted." *(Abu Dawud)*.

- Those who come late to the *Jama'at* (congregational prayer) should stand shoulder to shoulder with the person beside them. Then recite the *Takbir* standing, even if the *Imam* is in *Ruku* or in any other position '. Then recite another *Takbir* and assume the same position as the *Imam* is in. If he is in *Ruku* and you reach the position of the *Ruku* before he rises from it, you should consider yourself as having prayed that whole *Rak'ah*; but if you join after the *Ruku*, then you will have to pray it after the *Imam* finishes.

- If you miss one or more *Rak 'ah* with the *Imam*, follow him until the end of the *Salat*, but do not make *Taslim* when he does. Instead, stand up and offer the remaining *Rak'ahs* (that you missed).

- Beware of performing *Salat* in a rush, because it may not be accepted by Allah.

- If you forgot to perform an action which is *Wajib* (compulsory) in the *Salat*, like sitting at the end of the second *Rak 'ah* to recite *Tahiyyat*, or if you are unsure how many *Rak 'ahs* you prayed, then decide on the lower number (which is the number you are sure of) then at the end of the *Salat* make two extra *Sajdahs*. These are called *Sujud As-Sahw* (the prostrations for forgetfulness).

The holy Prophet (peace & blessings of Allah be with him) said:

- "The key to *Salat* is purity. It starts with the *Takbir* and it ends with the *Taslim.*" *(Tirmidhi)*

- *Qiyam* (standing) in obligatory *Salat*; Allah said:

"Guard strictly the (five obligatory) prayers, especially the middle *('Asr)* prayer. And stand before Allah with obedience (and do not speak to others during the prayers)." *(Q.2:238)*

Nafl (voluntary) *Salat*, can be offered sitting, even if one is able to stand. The Prophet (peace & blessings of Allah be with him) said:

"A man's *Salat* while sitting has half (the reward) of the (normal) *Salat*."

Those who are unable to stand for *Fard Salat*, they should pray sitting, and if unable to pray sitting, they should pray reclining on their side or as best as they can.

The parts of the body on which *Sajdah* must be made are: the face (i.e. nose and forehead), both hands, both knees, and the toes of both feet. The Apostle of Allah (peace & blessings of Allah be with him) said:

"I was ordered to make *Sajdah* on seven parts of the body; the forehead - (and he pointed to his nose) -both hands, both knees, and the toes of both feet."

The proper order of the prayer: Begin with *Takbirat-ul-Ihram* standing, recite *Al Fatihah*, then bow in *Ruku*, then rise up from it to standing, then perform *Sajdah*, then rise up from it to sitting, then perform the second *Sajdah*. In the second *Rak ah* and in the final *Rak'ah*, one should sit for *Tashahhud*, and after the final *Rak'ah* recite *Darud Shareef* and make *Taslim*.

Conditions For The VALIDITY of SALAT

The following conditions must be met before the beginning of the *Salat*, and if anyone of these is missing, the *Salat* will be invalid:

- Knowledge that the time for a particular *Salat* has begun. It is sufficient to be reasonably certain.
- To be in a state of purity, cleansed of the major and minor impurity. The Messenger of Allah (peace & blessings of Allah be with him) said:

"Allah will not accept *Salat* without purification." (*Muslim*).

- Cleanliness of one's body, clothing, and place of prayer if one is in a position to do so. If one is unable to remove the impurity, he may pray in whatever state he is in.

- Covering one's private parts; The private parts of men to be covered for offering Salat extend from the navel to the knees.

The private parts of women consist of all her body, other than the face and hands (in *Salat*). It is mandatory that the clothing should conceal the private parts. Any apparel that reveals the skin is not good enough, and the *Salat* is not acceptable in it.

- The *Niyah* (intention). The person about to pray should know what *Salat* he's going to pray - whether *Fardh* (obligatory) or *Nafl* (voluntary); and which prayer of the day - *Dhuhr* or *'Asr* etc.

- The worshipper should face the *Qiblah*, which is the Sacred Mosque in Makkah, as the holy Book says:

"So turn your face in the direction *of Al-Masjid-al-Haram* (at Makkah). And wheresoever you people are, turn your faces (in prayer) in that direction..." *(Q.2:144)*

One who is close enough to the Ka'bah to see it, must look at it before beginning his prayer to make sure that he is really facing it. And one who cannot see it must face in its direction, since that is the most he is capable of.

- Facing the *Qiblah* in *Salat is* an obligation that may not be waived except under the following circumstances:

- Voluntary *Salat of* a traveler mounted on an animal or any conveyance: a car, ship, plane, etc. The person can pray in whatever direction he is facing; and *if* sitting, he can make a gesture indicative *of Ruku'* and *Sajdah*. The lowering *of* his head in *Sajdah* should be more distinct than in *Ruku'*.

- One who fears (of present danger) or one held against his will in a certain position or direction, or one so weak, from illness that he cannot turn towards the *Qiblah*. In all of these cases the requirement of facing the *Qiblah* is waived due to inability.

TIMES During Which SALAT is Forbidden

- After the obligatory *Salat* of *Fajr* (Dawn) until the time when sun has risen.
- At the moment the sun is cresting the horizon until it reaches a spear's length above it (5° - 100).
- At high noon until it passes the zenith by a few minutes.
- After the obligatory *Salat* of *'Asr* (Afternoon) until the sun sets.

The Prophet (peace & blessings of Allah be with him) said:

"No *Salat* (prayer) is valid after the *'Asr* Prayer till the sun sets and no *Salat* (prayer) is valid after the *Fajr* Prayer till the sun rises."

- It is permissible to offer a *Salat*, one had previously forgotten or slept through, at any time; based on the Prophet's statement:

"Whoever forgot *a Salat* or slept through it, its expiation is that he offers it when he remembers it." *(Muslim)*

- Imam Ash-Shafeyi was of the opinion that it is permissible to pray a voluntary *Salat* that has a specific cause during the forbidden times, for instance two Rak'ahs as a greeting to the mosque whenever one enters into it and before sitting there; or two *Rak'ahs* after *Wudhu'*.

When it is announced that the obligatory *Salat* in congregation is about to be prayed (i.e. the Iqamah is recited), it is not permissible to occupy oneself with voluntary *Salat*.

The Prophet (peace & blessings of Allah be with him) said:

"When the *Salat* in congregation commences, there is no *Salat* other than the prescribed one (i.e. the obligatory *Salat* in the congregation)." *(Muslim)*.

The TIMES of Obligatory *SALAT*

Each *Salat* has a prescribed time in which it must be performed. Allah says in the Holy Book:

"...Verily the *Salat* is enjoined on the believers at fixed hours." (Q.4:103)

The Qur'an indicated these times in a general way, and the *Sunnah* explained them in detail. Abdullah bin 'Amr reported that the Messenger of Allah said:

"The time of *Dhuhr* (the Noon Prayer) is when the sun passes the zenith, until the shade of a man equals his length upon which the time for *'Asr* commences. And the time of *'Asr* (the Afternoon Prayer) is as long as the sun's light has not turned yellow. And the time of *Maghrib* (the Sunset Prayer) lasts as long as the redness has not vanished from the sky. And the time of *Isha'* (the Night Prayer) is until the middle of the night. And the time of *Fajr* (the Dawn Prayer) is from the first appearance of dawn (and lasts) as long as the sun has not yet risen. If the sun starts to crest the horizon, (then *Salat* is forbidden)."

From this *Hadith* and others it becomes clear that the times of *Salat* are as follows:

Fajr: starts with the appearance of the "true dawn" until the sun starts to crest the horizon.

Dhuhr: starts right after the sun passes its zenith, and continues until the shadow of an object equals the same length as the object.

'Asr: starts as soon as the shadow of the object becomes equal to the object after deducting the length of the shadow at noon. And it lasts until the sun sets (although it should not be postponed until the sun's rays turn yellowish without a valid excuse).

Maghrib: starts when the sun disappears below the horizon, and extends until the last trace of redness disappears from the sky.

'Isha': starts when the last trace of redness has disappeared from the sky, and lasts until the middle of the night.

The SALAT of the holy PROPHET

There are many *Ahadith*, either in words of the Prophet (peace & blessings of Allah be with him) or his companions' descriptions of his *Salat*, which throw light on how one should perform *Salat* in the best way. Some of these *Ahadith* are as follows:

Aswad ibn Yazid said: I asked 'Ayesha (may Allah be pleased with her) about the *Salat of* Allah's Messenger (peace & blessings of Allah be with him) during the night. She said:

"He used to sleep the first part of the night, then he would get up (and pray). Just before dawn he would offer *Witr*, and then come to bed... then when he heard the *Adhan* he would (leave his bed). If he was *Junub* (in a state of sexual impurity), he would take a bath, and if not, he would perform *Wudhu'*, then go out (to the mosque) for *Salat.* " *(Bukhari).*

The Apostle of Allah (peace & blessings of Allah be with him) reportedly said:

"What was made dear to me of your world (i.e. the worldly matters) is women and perfume; and the coolness of my eyes is in *Salat*" *(Ahmad).*

The Messenger of Allah (peace & blessings of Allah be with him) also said:

"When you stand to pray, perform a perfect *Wudhu'*, then face the *Qiblah;* say *Takbir* then recite what is easy for you from the Qur'an that is with you (i.e. memorized); then bow until you come to rest in *Ruku;* then rise up till you stand straight; then prostrate until you come to rest in *Sajdah* (prostration); then raise (your head) until you come to a sitting position; then prostrate until you come to rest in *Sajdah*. Then do that in all of your *Salat*."

"When the Prophet would stand up to offer *Salat*, he would raise his hands to the level of his shoulders. Then he would say *"Allahu Akbar"* until every bone came to rest in its place with him standing straight and upright Then he would recite. *"Allahu Akbar "*, raising his hands until they reached *the* level of his shoulders, then he would bow placing his palms on his knees, coming to rest without raising his head nor letting it droop. Then he would raise his head up saying: "Allah hears those who praise Him." Then he would raise his hands to the level of his shoulders, and say *"Allahu Akbar"* and then he would descend to the ground, keeping his hands away from his side. Then he would raise his head, with his left leg folded under him, sitting on it He would spread his toes (on the ground) when he would make *Sajdah*, then he would prostrate. After the *Sajdah* he would say *"Allahu Akbar"* raising his head and having his left leg folded under him, sitting on it until every bone had returned to its place. He would do the same in the second *Rak`ah* as he did in the first. When he would rise to stand after the first two *Rak`ahs*, he would say *"Allahu Akbar"* and raise his hands to the level of his shoulders, just as he did at the start of *Salat*, and he would perform the rest of the prayer like the first two *Rak`ahs*: Then when sitting after the last *Sajdah* before the *Taslim*, he would move his left leg back a bit so that he would be sitting on his left haunch." (Bukhari).

The Prophet (peace & blessings of Allah be with him) said:

"None of you should offer *Salat* in a single garment which leaves your shoulder bare." Muslim reported one version with the wording: "his two shoulders bare."

SALAT TA TA WWU' (Optional PRAYERS)

Optional *Salat* was prescribed to make up for deficiencies that might occur in obligatory *Salat;* and in view of the special merits of *Salat* in which other forms of worship are lacking. The Prophet (peace & blessings of Allah be with him) said:

"The first thing to be taken account of from the deeds of the slave on the Day of Judgment will be the *Salat*. If it is satisfactory, he will be successful and victorious; and if it is not so, he will fail and lose, and if something is deficient in his obligatory prayers, the Lord will say: 'Check if my slave has any optional *Salat* to his credit.' The deficiency will be made up from those. After that, the rest of his deeds will be examined in a similar way." (*Tirmidhi*)

The best place to offer voluntary *Salat* is in your own home. The Prophet (peace & blessings of Allah be with him) said:

"The best *Salat is* that of a man in his house, except for the obligatory *Salat*."

The Prophet (peace & blessings of Allah be with him) said:

"The *Salat* of a man in his house is more meritorious than his prayer in *my* mosque *(i.e.* the Prophet's Mosque in Madinah) except the obligatory *Salat*." *(Abu Dawud)*

Imam An-Nawawi said: "Stress was placed on praying optional *Salat* in the home because it further removes the chance of praying just to show off *(Ar-Riya)*, and it brings blessing to the house and mercy descends upon it as well as angels, and the Satan clears out."

In optional *Salat* it is permitted to sit even if one has the ability to stand, and it is also permissible to stand for part of it and sit for part, even in one *Rak'ah*. It makes no difference whether the sitting precedes the standing or vice versa.. And one can sit anyway he likes, although sitting cross-legged is the best. However, as the holy Prophet (peace & blessings of Allah be with him) remarked:

"The *Salat* of a man performed while sitting has half the (reward) of a *Salat (i.e.* performed while standing)." *(Muslim)*

Optional *Salat* encompasses the *Sunnah Salat* of *Fajr, Dhuhr,*

Asr, Maghrib and Isha', and Salat offered after Wudhu, and Tahajjud, and others.

SUJUD AS-SAHW

(Prostrations For FORGETFULNESS in the SALAT)

It is authentically proved that the Prophet (peace & blessings of Allah be with him) used to occasionally forget while he was in Salat. He said, instructing his followers:

"I am only a human being. I forget like you all forget, so if one of you forgets (in his Salat) he should prostrate twice (extra) in his (final) sitting." *(Ahmad)*

The two Sajdahs for forgetfulness: Prostrate twice either before the Taslim or after it. Both are authentically reported from the Prophet (peace & blessings of Allah be with him). He said:

"When one of you becomes uncertain in his Salat and does not remember how many (Rak'ahs) he prayed, three or four? He should cast away his uncertainty and stick to what he is sure about (i.e. the lesser number) then prostrate twice before the Taslim." *(Bukhari)*.

In the incident related to the companions known as Dhul-Yadain (where the Prophet (peace & blessings of Allah be with him) prayed two Rak'ahs instead of four, then completed the remaining Rak'ahs after his attention was invited to the lapse), he performed the Sujud As Sahw after the Taslim.

- It is preferable to try to follow the Sunnah as closely as possible, performing Sujud before the Taslim or performing Sujud after the Taslim in different situations as mentioned in the Ahadith, and in all other situations he has the choice.

The Prophet (peace & blessings of Allah be with him) said:

"If a person added to his *Salat* or detracted from it, he should perform two *Sajdahs.*" *(Muslim)*

The situations in which *Sujud As-Sahw* applies:

- If one makes *Taslim* before the completion of the *Salat*, he should stand, then complete the remainder, then perform two *Sajdah* at the end of the *Salat*.
- If one adds something to the *Salat*. The proof is:

The Prophet once prayed five *Rak'ahs*. He was asked, "Has an addition been made to the *Salat*?" He said, "Why do you ask that?" They said, "You prayed five *Rak'ahs*." Then he prostrated twice after (he had already made) the *Taslim*.

- If one forgets the first *Tashahhud*: The proof is:

"The Prophet led them in *Dhuhr* one day and in the second *Rak'ah* he stood up (after the second *Sajdah*) without sitting; the people stood up with him, until when the *Salat* was (almost) over and the people were awaiting the *Taslim*, he said the *Takbir* while sitting, then performed two *Sajdahs* before the *Taslim*, then made the *Taslim*. *(Bukhari)*.

And it is mentioned in a *Hadith* that one who forgot to sit for the *Tashahhud*, then remembers before he rises, he should return to the sitting posture; but if he is fully standing before he remembers, he should not sit back, but at the end of the *Salat*, he should perform the *Sujud As-Sahw*.

- If one is unsure how many *Rak'ahs* he prayed: The Prophet (peace & blessings of Allah be with him) said:

"If one of you becomes uncertain in his *Salat*, so that he doesn't know how much he prayed - three *Rak'ahs* or four - he should cast off what he is uncertain about, and consider only what he is sure of, then perform two *Sajdahs* before making the *Taslim*. So if he ends up praying five *Rak'ahs*, these (*Sajdahs*) will make his *Salat* even, and if he prayed correctly it is like rubbing the nose of Satan in the dust." *(Muslim)*

- If one is unsure how many *Rak'ahs* one has prayed, then it is advised to go with the lower number. The Prophet (peace & blessings of Allah be with him) said:

"If one of you is not sure between two and one, he should consider it as one *(Rak'ah)*; and if he is not sure between two and three, he should consider it as two; and if he's not sure between three and four, he should consider it as three. Because the uncertainty is in the extra *Rak'ah*. Then he should complete what is left of his *Salat* and perform two *Sajdahs* while sitting before he makes *Taslim*." *(Ahmad)*

Congregational Salat of women in the Mosque

It is permissible for women to go out to the mosque to participate in the daily congregational *Salat*, under the condition that they avoid clothing, ornaments, or perfume that will attract attention of the men or invite disorder and confusion.

The Prophet (peace & blessings of Allah be with him) said:

"Do not prevent the women from their share in the mosques when they seek your permission." *(Muslim)*

This *Hadith* indicates that a married woman should ask the permission of her husband and the unmarried should ask the permission of her father or guardian.

The Prophet (peace & blessings of Allah be with him) said:

"Any woman who puts on perfume should not attend `Isha' (night prayer) with us." *(Muslim)*

He (peace & blessings of Allah be with him) also said:

"Any woman who puts on perfume and goes to the mosque for prayers, her *Salat* will not be accepted until she washes (it off)." *(Ibn Majah).*

The Prophet (peace & blessings of Allah be with him) said:

"Do not forbid your women from (attending congregational

prayers in) the mosques, and their homes are better for them." *(Abu Dawud)*

This would suggests that the *Salat* of a woman in her house is better for her then her *Salat* in the mosque.

Prescribed dress for women in *Salat*

The Prophet (peace & blessings of Allah be with him) said:

"Allah will not accept the *Salat* of a woman who is of menstruating age except with *a Khimar (a* long scarf which covers her hair, neck, and chest)." *(Abu Dawud)*

This *Hadith* indicates that Allah will not accept the *Salat* of a woman who has attained puberty unless she covers her head and neck and wears a long dress which will cover her legs and feet, or wears socks which cover her feet and legs, so that nothing of her skin can be seen underneath them, in addition to a dress which covers her whole body. And it is permitted for her to expose her face and hands in *Salat* if there is no male stranger who can see her, as there is no proof which requires her to cover those parts in *Salat*.

The Role of Imam in a *SALAT*

The most deserving person to be Imam (the one who leads the *Salat)* should be the one who is most adept at reciting the Book of Allah. [This has two aspects: one is how much he has memorized the text of the Qur'an and knows its meanings, the other is how well he follows *Tajweed* (the rules of recitation)]. If they are equal in recitation, then the most learned in the *Sunnah;* if they are equal in that, then the one who is older.

The Prophet (peace & blessings of Allah be with him) said:

"The one who leads the people in *Salat* should be the most adept at reciting the Book of Allah; if they are equal in recitation, then the most learned in the *Sunnah*; and if they are equal in the *Sunnah*, then the one who made *Hijrah* earlier. And if they are equal in *Hijrah*, then the one who is older; and a man should certainly not lead where the other has authority, nor sit in his house on his furnishings without his permission." *(Muslim)*

- A child who has reached the age of discernment is eligible to be a *Imam*, since 'Amr bin Salamah used to lead people in *Salat* when he was six or seven years old because he knew more Qur'an than any of them.
- A blind man may lead *Salat*, since the Prophet appointed Ibn Umm Maktum as Governor of Al-Madinah in his absence, and he used to lead the people in *Salat*, and he was blind.
- A person praying *Fardh* (obligatory) *Salat* may lead a person offering *Nafl* (voluntary) *Salat* as it is permissible for a person offering *Nafl* to lead a person performing *Fardh*. This is based on the fact that Mu'adh used to pray *'Isha'* with the Prophet - then return to his tribe and lead them in the same *Salat*. So for him that *Salat* was optional or voluntary, and for them it was obligatory.
- A man who performed *Tayammum* can lead others in *Salat*. As 'Amr bin Al-A'as led people in *Salat* after performing *Tayammum* and the Prophet on learning about it did not object to it.
- A traveler ca be an *Imam* for a resident. The Prophet (peace & blessings of Allah be with him) led the people in *Salat* in Makkah at the time of its conquest, and he made all his prayers two *Rak'ah* except *Maghrib* and he said:

"O people of Makkah, stand and pray two more *Rak' ahs* because we are travelers."

If a traveler prays behind an *Imam* who is a resident, he must pray a complete *Salat* (four *Rak'ahs* for *Dhuhr*, *Asr* and *'Isha'*), even if he did not catch a full *Rak'ah* behind the *Imam*, before the *Imam* made *Taslim* (salutation).

- An *Imam*, who cannot stand, is allowed to pray sitting; the Prophet (peace & blessings of Allah be with him) said:

"The *Imam* is appointed in order to be followed, so when he says the *Takbir*, say the *Takbir* and do not say the *Takbir* until he does so. And when he goes into *Ruku'*, go into *Ruku'* and do not go to *Ruku'* until he does so; and when he says, "Allah hears those who praise Him", say, "Our Lord, and all praise is due to You"; and when he performs *Sajdah*, perform *Sajdah*, and do not perform *Sajdah* until he does so; and if he prays standing, pray standing and if he prays sitting all of you should pray sitting." *(Bukhari)*

'It is better for one who is being lead in prayer to pray standing when the *Imam* leads them sitting, as approved by the Prophet (peace & blessings of Allah be with him) during his last illness, when he prayed sitting and the people prayed standing. *(Fath Al-Bari, !:219)*

The MERITS of *SALAT*

Allah, Most High, says in the Holy Book:

> "And those who guard their prayers well, such shall dwell in the gardens (i.e. Paradise) honoured." (Q.70:34-35)

And Allah says:

> "...and offer prayers perfectly (Iqamat-as-Salat). Verily, prayer prevents from Al-Fahsha' (i.e. great sins of every kind, unlawful cohabitation, etc.) and Al-Munkar (i.e. disbelief, polytheism, and every kind of evil wicked deed etc.)..." (Q.29:45)

And Allah says:

> "So woe unto those performers of prayers (hypocrites), who delay their prayer from its fixed time." (Q.107:4-5)

And

> "Successful indeed are the believers. Those who offer their prayers with all solemnity and full submissiveness." (Q.23:1-2)

And

> "Then, there has succeeded them a posterity who have given up prayers (i.e. made their prayers to be lost, either by not offering them or by not offering them perfectly or by not offering them in their proper fixed times, etc.) And have followed lusts. So they will be thrown in Hell." (Q.19:59)

And the Prophet (peace & blessings of Allah be with him) said:

"What do you think if one of you had a river running past his door and he bathed in it five times a day, would any dirt remain on him?" They said, "No dirt would remain on him." He said, "Likewise is the similitude of the five daily prayers; with them Allah obliterates the sins."

The holy Prophet (peace & blessings of Allah be with him) also said:

"The covenant (which distinguishes) between us and them (non-Muslims) is *Salat*, so whoever abandons it has disbelieved" *(Ahmad)*

And he (peace & blessings of Allah be with him) said:

"Between a belief and *'Kufr* and *Shirk'* is the abandonment of the *Salat.* "*(Muslim)*

SALAT *in* Congregation and Friday Prayers

Congregational *Salat* five times a day and *Salat-ul-Jumu'ah* on Friday are obligatory on men and women based on the following evidence: Allah, the Most High, said:

> " O you who believe (Muslims)! When the call is proclaimed for the Salat (prayer) on the day of Friday (Jumu`ah prayer), come to the remembrance of Allah [Jumu`ah Khutbah (Friday sermon) and Salat (prayer)] and leave off business (and every other thing), that is better for you if you did but know!" (Q.62:9)

And the Prophet (peace & blessings of Allah be with him) said:

"Whoever leaves three *Jumu`ah* (prayers) consecutively, considering it not very important, Allah will seal his heart". *(Ahmad)*

And the Prophet (peace & blessings of Allah be with him) said:

"Whoever hears the *Adhan*, then does not come to the mosque (but prays at home), then he has no *Salat* (acceptable) unless he has an excuse (a valid one - for instance, fear or illness)." *(Ibn Majah).*

Abdullah ibn Mas'ud (may Allah be pleased with him) said:

"Whoever likes to meet Allah tomorrow as a Muslim, he should guard these five times daily *Salat* by praying them wherever the *Adhan* is called. Allah has prescribed for your Prophet (peace & blessings of Allah be with him) practices of guidance, and these prayers are from these practices of guidance. And if you pray in your homes, as some laggards do, you would abandon the *Sunnah* of your Prophet; and if you were to abandon the *Sunnah* of your Prophet, you will go astray. I witnessed a time when we used to see no one lagging behind from *Salat* in the mosque except the known *Munafiq* (hypocrite); and a sick person used to be helped to the mosque supported by two men, until he would stand in the row."

The Prophet (peace & blessings of Allah be with him) said:

"Whoever bathes, then comes to *Jumu`ah* (Friday prayer) then prayed whatever was written for him, then listened silently until the *Imam* finishes the *Khutbah* (sermon) then prays with the *Imam*, Allah will forgive his sins that he may have committed between the previous *'Jumu`ah* and the present one, plus three more days after that." *(Muslim)*

And he (peace & blessings of Allah be with him) said:

"Whoever performs a *Ghusl* (bath) on Friday, like the *Ghusl* for *Janabah* (state of sexual impurity) then proceeds to the mosque, it is as if he sacrificed a camel; and whoever sets out in the second time, it is as if he sacrificed a cow; and whoever sets out in the third time, it is as if he sacrificed a ram with horns; and the one who reached in the fourth time, it is as if he sacrificed a chicken; and whoever reaches in the fifth time, it is as if he has given an egg in charity; and, when the *Imam* comes out, the angels gather to listen to the sermon." *(Muslim)*

And he (peace & blessings of Allah be with him) said:

"Whoever prays `Isha' in congregation, it is as if he stood half the night (in *Salat);* and whoever prays *Fajr* (Dawn) in congregation, it is as if he stood the whole night." *(Muslim).*

And the Apostle of Allah (peace & blessings of Allah be with him) said:

"The *Salat* of a man in congregation excels his *Salat* in house or *Salat* in his shop (i.e. place of business) 23 to 29 times in reward. That is because when anyone performed *Wudhu',* and performed it well, then came to the mosque, with no other motive except the *Salat,* he takes no step without being raised thereby a degree, and a sin is removed from his account, until he enters the mosque. Once he enters therein he is counted as being in prayer as long as he waits for the *Salat,* and the angels keep praying for him as long as he is sitting where he prayed. They say, 'O Allah have mercy on him, O Allah forgive him, O Allah accept his repentance.' They do that as long as he bothers no one and as long as he keeps his *Wudhu".* *(Muslim)*

The Etiquettes of the FRIDAY PRAYER

- Take a bath on Friday, trim your nails, apply some scent and wear clean clothes after performing *Wudhu.*
- Do not eat raw onion or garlic and do not smoke. Clean your mouth with a *Siwak* (toothstick) or a toothbrush with toothpaste.
- Pray two *Rak'ahs* upon entering the mosque even if the *Khatib* (orator) is on the *Mimbar* (pulpit) in accordance with the guidance of the Prophet (peace & blessings of Allah be with him) who said:

"When you come for *Jumu'ah* and the *Imam* is giving the *Khutbah*, you should perform two *Rak ahs*, and make them short.")

- Sit quietly listening to the *Imam*.
- Pray the two obligatory *Rak ahs* of *Jumu'ah* behind the *Imam* (the intention should be in the heart).
- Pray four *Rak'ahs Sunnah*, afterwards, in the mosque or two *Rak'ahs* at home, which is better.
- Invoke the blessings of Allah for the holy Prophet (peace & blessings of Allah be with him). This should be more plentiful than on other days.
- Supplicate to Allah as much as you can on Friday. The Prophet (peace & blessings of Allah be with him) said:

"Verily, there is an hour on Friday that no Muslim catches while asking Allah for what is good in it, except that He (Allah) would give it to him."

The holy Prophet (peace & blessings of Allah be with him) said: "Pray as you have seen me praying." *(Bukhari)*

"When one of you enters the Mosque, he should pray two *Rak'ahs* before sitting down." (This prayer is called greeting of the Mosque). *(Bukhari)*

"Do not sit upon the graves and do not pray towards them." *(Muslim)*

"When the *Fardh* (obligatory) *Salat* starts, there is no *Salat* except the obligatory one." *(Muslim)*

"I was ordered not to pray with rolled up sleeves." *(Muslim)*

"Make your rows straight and get close together" *(Bukhari)*

"When the *Iqamah* of *Salat* is called, do not come to *Salat* rushing. Come walking calmly. Whatever you catch of the *Salat*, pray; and whatever you miss, complete it."

- When you perform *Sajdah*, place your hands down, and raise your elbows up." *(Muslim)*

"The first thing of the slave to be reckoned on the Day of Judgment will be his *Salat*. If it is good the rest of his deeds will be (accounted as) good. And if it is defective the rest of his deeds will be defective." *(Tabarani)*

The *SALAT* of a Traveler

Allah, Most High says:

"And when you (Muslims) travel in the land, there is no blame on you if you shorten your prayer..." *(Q. 4:101)*

Ibn Abbas said:

"Allah prescribed for you on the tongue of your Prophet four *Rak'ahs Salat* for a resident, two *Rak'ahs* during a journey and one *Rak'ah* in a state of fear (war)." *(Muslim)*

And the Prophet (peace & blessings of Allah be with him) said: "Shortening the prayer is a charity from Allah upon you, so accept this charity." *(Muslim)*

Ibn Al-Qayyim said: "The Prophet used to shorten four *Rak'ah Salat* when he would set out on a journey, praying them as two *Rak'ahs* until he returned to Al-Madinah, and it is not confirmed that he ever prayed four *Rak'ahs Salat* complete during a journey.

Joining two *Salat*: It is permissible for a traveler to pray *Dhuhr* and *'Asr* together, either by offering *'Asr* earlier (in the time of *Dhuhr*) or delaying *Dhuhr* (until the time of *Asr*), and in the same way, he can join *Maghrib* and *'Isha'*. This is permissible in the following circumstances:

- During *Hajj*, at Arafat and Muzdalifah. Scholars of religion agree that *Dhuhr* and *'Asr* should be prayed together during the time of *Dhuhr* at Arafat; and that *Maghrib* and *'Isha'* should be prayed together at the time of *'Isha'* at Muzdalifah; that is the proven *Sunnah* of the Prophet (peace & blessings of Allah be with him).

- Joining two *Salat* during a journey in the time of one of them is permissible, as is proven by the statement of Anas ibn Malik that:

"When the Prophet would travel before the sun passed the zenith, he would delay *Dhuhr* until the time of *'Asr*, then he would pray both together. And if the sun passed the zenith before he set out, he would pray *Dhuhr*, then mount his animal to travel."

Abu Nu'aim reported:

"When the Prophet (peace & blessings of Allah be with him) was on a journey he used to pray *Dhuhr* and *'Asr* together if the sun passed the zenith, and then he would set out."

The last *Hadith* indicates that joining two *Salat* during the time of the earlier one is permissible. The *Hadith* before that indicates the permissibility of delaying *a Salat* to join it to the one next to it.

Salat is allowed on ship or train or plane, in a manner it may be easy to perform, and it is permissible to join two *Salat* on them. The Prophet (peace & blessings of Allah be with him) was asked about *Salat* in a boat. He (peace & blessings of Allah be with him) said:

"Pray standing, unless you fear it might cause you to drown."

SALAT of THE SICK

Salat is mandatory even in a state of sickness, and for the *Mujahideen* during war. *Salat* brings an inner tranquility to the sick person which may help him get well.

And it is better for a sick person if his life is drawing to an end, to die as one who prays, and not to die disobedient by abandoning *Salat*. And Allah has made things easy for the sick person. He can make *Tayammum* if he cannnot use water for *Wudhu'* and *Ghusl* so that he doesnot abandon *Salat*.

- It is obligatory for the sick person to purify himself with water, that is to perform *Wudhu'* for the minor ritual impurity (passing wind or urine or answering the call of nature) and to perform a *Ghusl* for the major ritual impurity (sexual discharge).
- If he is unable to use water for purification due to his weakness or he fears aggravation in his condition that his recovery may be delayed, then he must perform *Tayammum*.
- If he is unable to perform the purification act by himself, someone should help him perform *Wudhu'* or *Tayammum*.
- If he has a wound on one of his limbs (which are washed for the purification act) he should wash it with water. If washing with water affects him (adversely) then he can wipe over the affected area with his wet hand. If wiping also affects him, then he should perform *Tayammum*.
- If he has a bandage or cast over some portion of his limbs, he should wipe over it with a wet hand in place of washing the limb and he doesn't need to perform *Tayammum* since the wiping took the place of washing.
- It is obligatory for the sick person to clean his body of physical filth. If he is unable, he should go ahead and pray in whatever condition he may be in and his *Salat* is valid. Also, he does not have to repeat the *Salat* later.
- It is obligatory for the sick person to pray in clean clothes. If physical filth gets on his clothes, he must wash it off or change into clean clothes. If he is unable to do so, he should pray as he is and his *Salat* is valid. In this situation he doesnot have to repeat the *Salat* later.
- It is obligatory for the sick person to pray on something clean, if the place becomes impure. It is obligatory to wash the place, or replace it with something clean, or put something clean over it. If he is unable to do so, he should pray as he is and his *Salat* is valid. In this situation he doesnot have to repeat the *Salat* later.

- It is not permitted for the sick person to postpone the *Salat* because he is too weak to purify himself. Rather he should purify himself as much as he is able to, and perform the *Salat* in its time, even if there is some filth on his body or clothes or his place that he is incapable of cleaning.

- It is obligatory for the sick person to pray standing, even if leaning, or propped up against a wall or on a crutch or staff, if he needs the support.

- If he cannot stand, he should pray sitting, and the best thing is for him to sit cross-legged in the positions of *Qiyam* and *Ruku'*.

- If he cannot sit, he should lie on his side, facing the *Qiblah*; and the right side is better to lie on. If he cannot manage to face the *Qiblah*, he should face wherever he is facing, and his *Salat* is valid, and he need not repeat it later.

- If he cannot offer the *Salat* lying on his side, he should lie on his back with his feet towards the *Qiblah* and if he is able, it is better for him to have his head propped up a bit so that his face is towards the *Qiblah*; again, if he cannot get his feet facing the *Qiblah*, he should pray wherever he is facing and he need not repeat the *Salat* later.

- It is obligatory for the sick person to perform *Ruku'* and *Sajdah* in his *Salat*. If he is unable, he can make a gesture with his head, making the gesture for *Sajdah* more prominent than the gesture for *Ruku'*. If he is able to perform *Ruku'* but not *Sajdah*, he should perform *Ruku'* normally then make the substitute gesture for *Sajdah*. And if he is able to perform *Sajdah*, he should perform *Sajdah* where called for and make the substitute gesture for *Ruku*, and it is not necessary to get a pillow to perform *Sajdah* on.

- If he cannot move his head, he should make the signal for *Ruku'* and *Sajdah* with his eyes, lowering his eyelids slightly for *Ruku'*, and more for *Sajdah*. As for gesturing with one's finger, as some sick people do, it is not considered valid.

- If he is unable to make a gesture with his head nor with his eyes, he should pray in his heart; saying *Takbir* and reciting, and making intention for *Ruku'* and *Sajdah* and standing and sitting in his heart.

- It is mandatory for the sick person to pray every *Salat* at its appointed time, and to perform every act of it according to his ability. If it proves difficult for him to pray each *Salat* on time, he can join *Dhuhr* and *'Asr*, and *Maghrib* and *'Isha'* together by delaying the first or offering the second earlier, whatever is easier for him. As for *Fajr*, it must be prayed at its regular time, without joining it to what is before it nor to what is after it.

- If the sick person travels for medical treatment to another country or city, he may shorten his four *Rak'ah Salat*, praying *Dhuhr*, *Asr* and *Isha*, each as two *Rak'ahs*, until he returns to his own place, whether the period of his journey is long or short.

SUPPLICATIONS during *SALAT*

The following supplications have been recommended before the time of prayer:

- O Allah, place a distance between my sins and me, like the distance you placed between the east and the west. O Allah forgive me of my sins like the white robe is purified from dirt. O Allah, wash my sins with water, snow and hail.

[The holy Prophet-peace & blessings of Allah be with him- used to recite this before the *Fardh Salat*].

- O Allah, you are the King, none has the right to be worshipped but You, You are my Lord, and I am Your slave. I wronged my soul and I admit my sin, so forgive me of all my sins. Indeed, no one forgives sins except You. O Allah, guide me to the best character, none can guide to the best of it except You, and divert from me the evil (character), for verily none can divert from me the evil of it except You". *(Muslim)*

[The holy Prophet (peace & blessings of Allah be with him) used to recite it before the *Fardh* and *Nafi Salat*].

The following supplications are recommended after the *Salat*.

- O Allah, verily I seek refuge with You from the torment of Hell, and from the torment of the grave, and from the trial of life and death and from the evil of the trial of the *Dajjal* (*the* Antichrist)." *(Muslim)*

[The Messenger of Allah (peace & blessings of Allah be with him) used to recite it after *Tashahhud*].

- O Allah, I seek refuge with you from the evil of what I have done and from the evil of what I have not done." *(Nasa'i)*

SALAT at the Funeral

Make the intention for Funeral *(Janazah)* Prayer in your heart and recite four *Takbirs*.

- After the first *Takbir*, say *A'udhu billahi* ... i.e.I seek refuge with Allah from Satan and say *Bismillahir Rahmanir Rahim* then recite *Surah Al-Fatihah*.

- After the second *Takbir*, recite *Salat-ul-Ibrahimia* on the Prophet just as you do in *Salat*:

اَللَّهُمَّ صَلِّ عَلَى مُحَمَّدٍ وَّعَلَى اٰلِ مُحَمَّدٍ كَمَا صَلَّيْتَ عَلَى اِبْرَاهِيْمَ وَعَلَى اٰلِ اِبْرَاهِيْمَ اِنَّكَ حَمِيْدٌ مَّجِيْدٌ ۔ اَللَّهُمَّ بَارِكْ عَلَى مُحَمَّدٍ وَّعَلَى اٰلِ مُحَمَّدٍ كَمَا بَارَكْتَ عَلَى اِبْرَاهِيْمَ وَعَلَى اٰلِ اِبْرَاهِيْمَ اِنَّكَ حَمِيْدٌ مَّجِيْدٌ ۔

O Allah, have mercy on and reward Muhammad and the family of Muhammad as You had mercy and rewarded Ibrahim ... etc."

"After the third *Takbīr* supplicate the following *Du'a'* reported from the Prophet (peace & blessings of Allah be with him):

O Allah, forgive our living and our dead, and those of us present and those of us who are absent, and our young and our old, and our male and female. O Allah, whomsoever You caused to live among us, make them live in Islam, and those whom You cause to die among us, make them die in *Iman* (belief). O Allah, do not hold back from us his reward, and do not test us after him." (*Tirmidhi*)

- After the fourth *Takbir*, supplicate as you wish, then end with *Salam* to the right.

EID PRAYERS

"The Prophet (peace & blessings of Allah be with him) used to go out to a designated area for *Salat* on the festival at the end of Ramadhan (*'Eid ul-Fitr*) and the feast of the sacrifice (*'Eid ul Adh-ha"*), and the first thing he would start with would be the *Salat*."(*Bukhari*)

The Prophet (peace & blessings of Allah be with him) said:

"The number of *Takbirs* for the *Salat* of *'Eid ul Fitr* is seven in the first *Rak'ah* and five in the second, then recitation after them in both *Rak'ahs*." (*Abu Dawud*)

Salat of the two *'Eid* (festivals) is part of the religion and it is two *Rak'ahs*. One should say seven *Takbir* in the beginning of the first *Rak'ah* and five in the beginning of the second *Rak'ah*. Then recite *Al-Fatihah* and thereafter whatever is easy.

The Messenger of Allah (peace & blessings of Allah be with him) said:

"Verily, the first thing we start with on this day (*Eid al-Adh-ha*) of ours is *Salat*, then we go back and sacrifice an animal. Whoever did so, he has acted according to our *Sunnah*. And whoever slaughters before the prayer, it is only meat he provided for his family, and it is not part of the rites (of *Adh-ha*) in the least."

And he (peace & blessings of Allah be with him) said:

"O people, on every house there is a sacrifice (due)." *(Ibn Majah)*.

And he (peace & blessings of Allah be with him) said:

"Whoever has the means to sacrifice but does not do so, then he should not come near our place of *Eid* prayer." *(Ahmad)*

SALAT-UL ISTIKHARAH
(Prayer to seek divine guidance)

Jabir (may Allah be pleased with him) said:

The Prophet (peace & blessings of Allah be with him) used to teach us *Istikharah* in all affairs in the way he would teach us a *Surah* of the Qur'an. He would say:

If one of you is concerned about something and is in need of guidance from Allah, he should pray two *Rak'ahs* of optional *Salat*, then say:

'O Allah, verily I seek the good from You by Your Knowledge, and I seek the Decree from You by Your Power and I ask You of Your immense bounty. Because You are able and I am not, and You know and I do not know; and You are the Total Knower of the unseen.

'Oh Allah, if You know this affair (and it should be mentioned) is good for me, in my religion and my livelihood and the final outcome of my affairs (or he said: In my immediate affairs and my long term ones) then decree it for me, and make it easy for me, and bless me in it, and if You know this affair (and the affair should be mentioned) is evil for me in my religion and my livelihood and in the final outcome of my affairs (or he said: In my immediate affairs and my long term ones), then divert it away from me, and divert me away from it, and decree for me the good wherever it may be, then make me content with that." *(Bukhari)*

This *Salat* and *Du 'a'* should be prayed by the person for himself with the certainty that his Lord, Whom he consulted for the right choice, will direct him to what is best for him. And the sign that the thing is good is that Allah will make the means of its attainment easy for him.

SIYAM
(Fasting)

SIYAM
(Fasting)

O you who believe, fasting is prescribed for you as it was prescribed for those before you in order that you may be conscious of Allah... Ramadhan is the (month) in which the Qur'an was revealed as a guide to mankind and as a clear evidence for guidance and judgment (between right and wrong). So whoever among you witness this month, let him spend it in fasting; but if anyone is ill or on a journey, the prescribed period (should be made up) by days later. Allah intends ease for you and He does not intend hardship, and (He desires) that you should complete the prescribed period, and that you may glorify Allah for guiding you and that you may be thankful (Q. 2: 183-185).

Islam recognises that the physical needs and appetites, particularly those of food, drink and sex, are powerful factors in human life, tying man to dependence on and preoccupation with the bodily needs and desires. Hence the Muslim is asked for one month each year to do without the satisfaction of these needs by day in order to develop his spiritual nature. The process of experiencing hunger, thirst and sexual abstinence is likely to have the effect of weaning away human beings from dependence on physical satisfaction and the dominance of their animal needs, freeing them to pursue spiritual goals and values during this period. During the month of Ramadhan Muslims have the opportunity to devote themselves to Allah and to their spiritual development.

Fasting makes the Muslim disciplined, steadfast and resilient. It trains him to be flexible and adaptable in his habits, capable of enduring hardship, and not to take for granted the bounties of Allah. Fasting also enables the Muslim to feel with the poor who experience hunger daily and to be active in compassion and charity towards them.

Fasting, in Islam, is not related to penance for sins or as a means of appeasing the wrath of the Lord, as in some other religions; it is total abstinence from all food, drink and marital relations throughout the daylight hours. Fasting, in Islam, is not an ascetic or self-mortifying practice but an act of self-discipline and obedience to Allah.

The Qur'an describes the purpose of fasting as 'self-restraint' and the holy prophet (peace & blessings of Allah be with him) described it as 'a shelter'. Fasting is a shelter in the sense that the fasting individual knows he should avoid the evil of his or her human nature. The fasting Muslim learns, in particular, that food and drink are indeed precious gift from Allah.

However, mere abstinence from food and drink is not the real meaning of fasting. The holy prophet (peace & blessings of Allah be with him) reportedly said: Allah does not accept the fasting of those who do not restrain themselves from telling falsehood, or from doing false deeds.

And he (peace & blessings of Allah be with him) also said:

Allah will pardon all the sins of those who fast during

Ramadhan out of true belief and in anticipation of Allah's Reward in the Hereafter.

Fasting is an effective means to establish the control of the spirit over the body, where humans live with full control over themselves, without being slaves to their physical inclinations or needs.

Every day of the month of *Ramadhan* is a day of fasting. And fasting is obligatory on all Muslims past puberty, with the following exceptions:

Sick person for whom fasting may be hazardous, Travellers for whom fasting would involve hardship; women during menstruation and up to forty days following childbirth, pregnant women and nursing mothers if fasting is likely to harm the mother or infant; the very old and the insane. The latter two categories are permanently exempt from fasting, while the others are exempt only for the duration of their condition, and must make up the missed fasts at any time before the beginning of the next Ramadhan if possible.

If one has a permanent condition that makes fasting impossible or hazardous to health, he or she is permitted, instead to give needy person alms equivalent to one meal for each day he or she did not fast.

Allah, Most High, said:

> you who believe, fasting is prescribed for you as it was prescribed for those before you that you may achieve Taqwa." (Q.2:183).

(*Taqwa* is translated as piety or as consciousness of Allah, or as fear of Allah. It is derived from the word *Wiqayah* for "Shield". According to some scholars this means to shield yourself from Allah's wrath by hurrying to do what He ordered you and by strictly avoiding what He has prohibited).

And the Messenger of Allah (peace & blessings of Allah be with him) said:

"Siyam (fasting) is a shield (or a screen or a shelter) from Hell-fire."

He (peace & blessings of Allah be with him) also said:

"Whoever observed fasting during Ramadhan with perfect faith and seeking reward, he will have his previous sins forgiven."

"Whoever stood to pray *(Tarawih)* in Ramadhan with perfect faith and seeking reward, he will have his previous sins forgiven."

Allah has made fasting obligatory, and it is an act of worship, and it has many benefits, such as:

- Fasting gives the digestive organs a rest, and causes the body to get rid of accumulated wastes which are detrimental to health. It strengthens the body and is beneficial for the treatment of many diseases. It also presents an opportunity for smokers to break their addiction since they cannot smoke during the day.

- Fasting is training for the self, getting it used to good deeds, discipline, obedience, patience and sincerity.

- The fasting person feels one with all his fasting brethren; he fasts with them and breaks fast with them, and he experiences the general Islamic unity. He experiences hunger that should make him empathise with his brethren who are hungry and needy.

Essential PRACTICES during RAMADHAN

Allah has made fasting obligatory on all Muslims as a way to worship Him. For the fasting to be acceptable and beneficial, the following is required to be observed.:

- Guard the *Salat*. Fasting persons should perform obligatory *Salat* regularly for it is a pillar of the religion and abandoning it is an act of disbelief.

- Be well mannered. Beware of disbelief, cursing the religion, treating people badly, and using the fast as an excuse. Fasting is to train the self, not to ruin the manners, and disbelief puts a Muslim outside his faith.

- Do not use foul or harsh language even while joking, as it may diminish (the reward of) the fast. The Prophet (peace & blessings of Allah be with him) has said:

"If one of you is fasting, he should not use obscenity that day nor shout; and if someone speaks abusively or wants to fight with him, he should say: `Verily I'm fasting, verily I'm fasting."

- Take advantage of fasting to give up smoking. Smoking is injurious to health.

- Do not overeat at the time of breaking the fast, as the benefit of fasting is cancelled and it is not healthy.

- Do not waste your time by going to movies or watching television.

- Do not stay up so late at night that you are not able to wake up for *Sahur* (the predawn meal) or *Salat-ul-Fajr*, or go to work in the morning. The Prophet (peace & blessings of Allah be with him) said:

"O Allah, bless my *Ummah* in their early mornings (acts)." *(Ahmad).*

- Increase spending in charity on relatives and the needy. Visit your relatives, and make peace with those with whom you have had disputes.

- Increase your remembrance of Allah, recitation of Qur'an, listening to it, and contemplation of its meanings. Practise *I'tikaf* (secluding oneself for the purpose of worship) in the Mosque at the end of Ramadhan (this is *Sunnah*).

- Be reverential of the fast of Ramadhan. Beware of breaking the fast without a valid excuse. Whoever does so must repent for that and make up for that day, and whoever has intercourse with his wife during the daytime of Ramadhan he has to expiate the sin. He should fast two months continuously (60 days without missing a day); and if he cannot do that, he should feed 60 poor persons one meal.

Allah's Messenger (peace & blessings of Allah be with him) reortedly said:

Whoever does not abstain from deceitful speech and actions, Allah is not in need of him leaving off his food and drink. *(Bukhari)*.

It is recommended to break the fast with dates, because it is a blessed fruit. And if dates are not available, then break it with water, because Allah's Messernger said that water purifies. *(Tirmidhi)*.

ªThe Prophet (peace & blessings of Allah be with him) used to recite at the time of *Iftar:*

" O Allah I kept the fast for You, and with Your sustenance I am breaking (my fast). The thirst is gone, and the veins replenished, and the reward is confirmed, if Allah wills," *(Abu Dawud)*

And the Prophet (peace & blessings of Allah be with him) said:

"The people will continue to be upon goodness as long as they hurry to *Iftar* (break fast after the sun sets)."

And the Prophet (peace & blessings of Allah be with him) said:

"Take *Sahur* (predawn meal), for verily in the *Sahur* there is blessing."

The VIRTUES of FASTING

The Messenger of Allah (peace & blessings of Allah be with him) said:

"When Ramadhan begins, the doors of heaven are opened, the doors of Hell are closed and the devils are chained up." And in another version: "When Ramadhan starts, the doors of Paradise are opened." And in another version: "The doors of mercy are opened."

According to the holy Prophet (peace & blessings of Allah be with him), Allah, Most High, has said:

Every good deed of the son of Adam is multiplied in reward 10 to 700 times except for fasting, for it is for Me and I will grant the reward for it. He (the fasting person) leaves his passion and his food for My sake. The fasting person has two moments of happiness: One moment when he ends his fasting for the day *(Iftar)* and the other when he meets his Lord. And the smell, which issues from the mouth of the fasting person, is more pleasant to Allah than the smell of musk (fragrance).

Voluntary FASTING

The Prophet (peace & blessings of Allah be with him) used to encourage fasting in certain other days other than *Ramadhan*.

- During the first Six days in Shawwal (the month after *Ramadhan*).

The Prophet (peace & blessings of Allah be with him) said:

"Whoever fasts (during the month of) *Ramadhan*, then follows it up with six days in *Shawwal*, it is as if he fasted the whole (year)." *(Muslim)*

Some scholars believe that the reward of good deeds is multiplied by ten. 30 x 10 = 300 + [6 days x 10] = 360 which is slightly longer than a lunar year, and next Ramadhan he will fast again so it is as if he fasted his whole life.

- Fasting during the first ten days of Dhul-Hijjah and the day of 'Arafah (the 9th day of Dhul-Hijjah) (for those who are not performing *Hajj*); the Prophet (peace & blessings of Allah be with him) said:

- "Fasting on the day of *'Arafah* expiates two years of sins, last year's and next year's and fasting on the tenth day of Muharram *('Ashura)* expiates the previous year's." *(Muslim).*
- Fasting on the day of *'Ashura'*, along with one day before it, or one day after it. The Prophet (peace & blessings of Allah be with him) said:

"Today is the day of *'Ashura'*, and its fasting is not mandatory on you, and I am fasting, so whoever wants should fast, and whoever wants should break his fast."

- Fasting during the month of Sha'ban. It is reported that Allah's Messenger (peace & blessings of Allah be with him) used to fast most of *the month of Sha'ban*.
- Fasting on Monday and Thursday. The Prophet (peace & blessings of Allah be with him) explained that:

"Concerning fasting on Monday and Thursday, the deeds of the worshippers are presented before Allah on Monday and Thursday, and I like my deeds to be presented while I am fasting." *(Nasa'i).*

He was asked about fasting on Monday, he said: "That is the day I was born and the day (the first Revelation) was sent down on me." *(Muslim).*

- Fasting the 13th, 14th and 15th of every lunar month.

One of the companions said:

"The Prophet instructed us to fast the three days of whiteness *(Ayam ul-Beedh)* every month, the 13*th*, 14th and 15*th*." *(Nasa'i)*

THINGS that BREAK the FAST

The things that break the fast are of two categories:

I. What breaks the fast and requires only making up for it *(Qadha).*

II. What breaks it and requires making up for it (*Qadha'*), and also performing an act of expiation (*Kaffarah*).

I What requires *Qadha'* only:

- To eat and drink, knowingly and intentionally.
- To induce vomiting intentionally, the Prophet said:

"Whoever induced vomiting must make up for (the fast)." (*Al-Hakim*).

- Menstruation and post-partum bleeding. Even if the bleeding starts just before the sun sets, that day's fasting must be repeated.
- Ejaculation, either by masturbation or any other method of ejaculating short of intercourse, whether the cause was kissing the wife, or hugging her, or by use of the hand, etc. This nullifies the fast but requires *Qadha'* only.

II. What requires *Qadha'* and *Kaffarah* both:

According to a majority of scholars it is only sexual intercourse during the time of fasting that requires both *Qadha'* (repeating) and *Kaffarah* (expiation). The expiation is to free a slave, or to fast two lunar months in succession without missing a day, or to feed sixty poor people. Some scholars say the obligation is in that order, i.e. first one should free a slave; then, if that's not possible, to observe fast; then, if that's not possible, to feed the poor. This rule applies to men and women equally.

Things Which DO NOT Blemish The FAST

- To eat or drink forgetfully or mistakenly, or due to another person's threats and compulsion. There is no necessity for *Qadha'* or *Kaffarah*. The holy Prophet (peace & blesssings of Allah be with him) said:

Siyam (Fasting)

"Allah has removed from my *Ummah* (the burden of) mistakes and forgetfulness and what they are forced to do against their wills". *(At-Tabarani)*

And according to another *Hadith* the Messenger of Allah (peace & blessings of Allah be with him) said:

"Whoever forgot while he was fasting and ate or drank he should complete his fast, for it was Allah Who fed him and gave him to drink".

- Unintentional vomiting. The Prophet (peace & blesssings of Allah be with him) said:

"Whoever is overcome by vomiting (i.e. he does so unintentionally) while fasting, there is no *Qadha'* on him." *(Al-Hakim)*

I'TIKAF
(To be Secluded for worship inside a Mosque)

According to the *Shari'ah*, *I'tikaf* means staying in the mosque with the intention of seeking nearness of Allah. All the scholars agree that it is *Mashru'* (a legitimate part of Islam) because:

"The Prophet used to stay in the mosque during the last ten days of Ramadhan until he died, then his wives used to do the same after him."

I'tikaf is of two kinds: Supererogatory *(Masnun)* and Compulsory *(Wajib)*.

The *Masnun* kind is what a Muslim does voluntarily, in order to seek nearness of Allah and to follow the *Sunnah* of the Messenger of Allah (peace & blessings of Allah be with him). This act of worship is especially recommended during the last ten days of Ramadhan.

The *Wajib I'tikaf* is what a person makes compulsory upon himself by a vow *(Nadhr)*.

The Etiquettes of *I'tikaf*:

It is reported that whenever the holy Prophet (peace & blessings of Allah be with him) intended to perform *I'tikaf*, he used to offer his *Fajr* prayers, then enter the area he selected for *I'tikaf* in the mosque.

Any one who desires to undertake *I'tikaf* should be a Muslim, having reached the age of discernment, purified from *Janabah*, menses and post-partum bleeding. He or she should make the intention of staying in the Mosque with the objective of seeking nearness of Allah. During the period of *I'tikdf* a person may go out from the place of *I'tikaf* to bid farewell to his family. He may go out of the Mosque for pressing necessities like using the toilet, or to eat and drink, if no one brings him food. It is permitted to eat and drink and sleep in the mosque with the proper care taken to maintain its cleanliness.

Hadrat Ayesha (may Allah be pleased with her) is reported to have said:

The *Sunnah* for one in *I'tikaf* is not to leave the mosque to visit the sick, nor to attend a burial, nor to touch a woman nor to have sex with her, and not to leave the mosque except for unavoidable need; and there is no *I'tikaf* without fasting; and there is no *I'tikaf* except in a mosque where *Jumu'ah* (Friday prayer) is established." *(Abu Dawud)*.

Things which nullify *I'tikaf*:

I'tikaf is nullified when one leaves the mosque without need, intentionally; or due to loss of rationality through insanity or drunkenness; and also if a woman is beset with menstruation and post-partum bleeding.

ZAKAT
(Poor-Due)

ZAKAT
(Poor-Due)

> *It is not righteousness that you turn your faces towards the East or the West, but righteousness is that one believes in Allah and the last Day and the Angels and the Book and the Prophet; and (that you) give your wealth out of love for Him, for Kinsmen, orphans, the needy, the traveler, those who ask, and to ransom captives; and (that you) establish Salat and give Zakat. And those who keep their commitments when they make them and are patient in tribulation and adversity and in the struggle. They are the truthful and they are Allah – conscious. (Q. 2:177).*

The obligation of *Zakat* has been mentioned repeatedly in the Qur'an in the same sentence as the obligation of *Salat* to underscore its being a fundamental duty of a Muslim, and a prescribed act of worship.

Zakat in Arabic means 'purification' and has no precise equivalent in the English language; the nearest meaning is "poor due".

Islam proclaims that the true owner of everything is Allah who bestows wealth on people out of His beneficence as He sees fit. Hence those who have been granted riches have an obligation to spend on those who need help. In concrete terms, *Zakat* consists of an amount, which is assessed on the non-essential property of the Muslim, to be distributed among:

> *'the poor and the needy, and those who work on it* (collecting zakat) *and those whose hearts are to be reconciled and* (to free) *captives and* (help) *debtors, and in the cause of Allah, and for travelers (Q. 9: 60).*

In addition to helping those who are in need or distress, *Zakat* funds may also be spent for the construction of mosques, religious schools and hospitals, (in the cause of Allah) and for the salaries of those involved in the propagation or study of Islam whose work denies them the opportunity to earn a livelihood.

Zakat is assessed at two and a half percent per year on cash or capital which is beyond one's immediate needs, as, for example, cash savings or investments, the inventory of business, cattle, lands and crops which are a source of profit and so on.

Zakat is not applicable on property that is for personal use such as clothes, furniture, house used for living, car, and crops planted for domestic consumption.

Zakat is called "purification" because all wealth belongs to Allah who gives it in trust to people as He sees fit, a part of what one possesses is to be returned back to Allah in this form.

Hence the payment of *Zakat*, which is the share of Allah and the Muslim community in the wealth of the Muslim, purifies his remaining possessions and makes his ownership of them legal and permissible. It also purifies his heart from greed and selfishness, and from regarding what Allah in His bounty has bestowed on him as solely his by right. At the same time *Zakat* purifies the heart of the one who receives it from envy and hatred of those who are better off. Rather than being the enemies or exploiters of the poor, the affluent are brothers-in-faith who acknowledge their right on what Allah has given them and, from His bounty, extend their help to the poor and the needy.

Zakat is in effect a form of social security in the Muslim society. It is an institutionalized, obligatory kind of sharing and caring which equalizes wealth in the community without, at the same time, banning private ownership of property or stipulating that all people must possess an equal amount of wealth. Zakat attempts to deal with the problems of inequality and at the same time offers a solution to class rivalries and hatreds.

The Qur'an warns those who refuse to give charity or Zakat:

> Let not those who covetously withhold of the gifts that Allah hath given them of His Grace, think that it is good for them:
>
> Nay, it will be worse for them. Soon shall the things that they covetously withheld be tied to their necks like a twisted collar on the Day of Judgment (Q. 3:180).

Scholars of Fiqh also claim that, for those who die before paying their dues of charity, such dues become a debt on their inheritance, which should not be distributed among the heirs unless the debt of Zakat is settled.

The IMPORTANCE of ZAKAT In ISLAM

Zakat is an obligatory charity due on the wealth of a Muslim. The holy Qur'an links Salat along with Zakat.. The holy Book proclaims:

"And offer prayers perfectly *(Iqamat-as-Salat)* and give Zakat..." (Q.2: 110)

And Allah, Most High, said:

> "And they were commanded not, but that they should worship Allah, and worship none but Him Alone

(abstaining from ascribing partners to Him), *and offer prayers perfectly* (Iqamat-as-Salat) *and give Zakat, and that is the right religion."* (Q.98: 5).

There is great wisdom in the institution of *Zakat*. It was mandated for many noble purposes such as the following:

- Purification of the believer's soul from the stains of sins and transgressions and their negative effects on the hearts, and the cleansing of his soul from the despicable qualities of miserliness and stinginess and their effects. Allah, Most High, says:

  "Take Sadaqah (alms) *from their wealth in order to purify them and sanctify them."* (Q.9: 103).

- To fulfill the needs of the poor Muslim and to preserve his honour from the humiliation of asking other than Allah.

- To lighten the burden of the Muslim debtor by helping to pay off his debts.

- To bring infirm hearts to belief and Islam, bringing them from a state of doubt, spiritual uneasiness and weak faith to firmly rooted faith and complete certainty.

- To assist those who strive in the way of Allah for the establishment of justice between the people so that religion (worship) be solely for Allah Alone in the entire world.

- Helping the stranded Muslim traveler to complete his journey.

- Purification of wealth and its increase, and protection from ruin through the blessing incurred by the obedience of Allah, and honouring of His order; and showing kindness to His creation.

WEALTH on which ZAKAT is Obligatory

Zakat is mandatory on four things:

- **The produce of the earth such as grains and fruits.**

The Holy Book reads:

"*O you who believe! Spend of the good things which you have (legally) earned, and of that which We have produced from the earth for you.*" *(Q.2:267)*

And :

"*...but pay the due thereof (its Zakat, according to Allah's orders 1/10th or 1/20th) on the day of its harvest...*" *(Q. 6:141).*

And the greatest of dues on wealth is the *Zakat,* the Prophet (peace & blessings of Allah be wit him) said:

"On a land irrigated by rain water or by natural water channels or if the land is wet due to a nearby water channel, *'Ushr (i.e.* one-tenth) is compulsory (as *Zakat);* and on the land irrigated by the well, half of the *'Ushr (i.e.* one-twentieth) is compulsory (as *Zakat)* on the yield of the land."

- **Gold, silver and money**.

The Holy Book reads:

"*...And those who hoard up gold and silver and spend it not in the way of Allah-announce unto them a painful torment.*" *(Q.9:34)*

And the holy Prophet (peace & blessings of Allah be wit him) said:

"There is no possessor of gold and silver who does not pay the due *(Zakat)* on them except that on the Day of Judgment, the gold and silver will be beaten into sheets of fire which will be further heated in the fire of Hell, then his flanks and forehead and back will be branded with them; every time they cool down they will be replaced with heated sheets. That will go on for a day which will last 50,000 years, until all the slaves have been judged." *(Sahih Muslim).*

- **Business inventory**:

That is, goods owned to be sold. This includes real estate, animals, foods, drinks, cars, etc. The owner should calculate their value at the end of his first year of business (and every year after that), and pay 2.5% of their current value, whether their value is the same as when he bought them or has gone up or down.

It is mandatory for the business owners like grocers, auto dealers, parts stores, to conduct a detailed account each year and pay the required *Zakat* on it. If that is hard on them, they can play it safe and pay enough to be sure they have discharged their responsibility.

- **Livestock:**

That is camels, cattle, sheep and goats, on the condition that they are free grazing, not fed with grain or specially prepared fodder, raised for breeding and milk production, and the number of head reaches the minimum payable level.

Some scholars are of the opinion that even if the cattle is fed with grain or special fodder, and is being raised for sale, *Zakat* must be paid on it, not because it is livestock but because it is a commodity for sale (the third category) payable at 2.5% of its sale value if it reaches the minimum payable value for merchandise (either by itself or in conjunction with other merchandise for sale).

The *NISAB* on which *ZAKAT* is DUE

- **Grains and fruit:**

Five *Awsuq* that is equal to 618 kilograms. The *Zakat* due is 10% on what is irrigated by rainfall, or springs, or other natural means, 5% if it is irrigated by methods that require labour and/or capital.

- **Gold, silver and currency**

Gold: 20 Dinars or 85 grams. The *Zakat due* is 2.5%.

Silver: 5 *Awaq* that equals 595 grams. The *Zakat* due is 2.5%.

Paper Money: The value of 85 grams of gold or 595 grams of silver in that currency.

- **Merchandise for sale:**

The value is calculated, and if it reaches the *Nisab* of gold or silver, *Zakat is* due on it at the rate of 2.5% of its value.

- **Livestock:**

Camels: the minimum *Nisab* is five camels. The *Zakat* due is a sheep.

Cattle: The minimum *Nisab* is 30 cows. The *Zakat* due is a one-year-old calf.

Sheep and goats: The minimum *Nisab* is 40 heads. The *Zakat* due is one sheep or one goat.

For free grazing Sheep and goats one livestock is due from 4o to 120. Two are due on 121 to 200. Three are due from 201 to 300. And one extra on every 100 livestock.

Billy goats and too old animals whose teeth have fallen out should not be given in *Zakat*.

Likewise a pregnant ewe or a female camel should not be given in *Zakat*.

Zakat Due on Camels

On 5 to 9 camels, *Zakat* due is one ewe (female camel).

On 10 to 14 camels, two ewes are due.

On 15 to 19 camels, three ewes are due.

On 20 to 24 camels, Four ewes are due.

On 25 to 35 camels, one 1-year-old female camel is due.

On 36 to 45 caamels, one 2-year-old female camel is due.

On 46 to 60 camels, one 3-year-old female camel is due.

On 61 to 75 camels, one 4-year-old female camel is due.

On 76 to 90 camels, two 2-year-old female camels are due.

On 91 to 120 camels, two 3-year-old female camels are due.

On 121 to 160 camels, three 2-year-old female camels are due as *Zakat*.

Thereafter for every forty camels, one extra 2-year-old camel is due; and for every extra fifty camels, one extra 3-year-old camel is due.

Zakat due on Cattle

On 30 to 39 cattle one-year-old cow is due.

On 40 to 59 cattle one two year old cow is due.

On 60 to 89 cattle two one year old cow are due.

Thereafter for every thirty extra heads, one extra 1-year-old cow is due and for every forty extra heads, one extra 2-year-old cow is due. ('*A Zakat Guide*' by *Adil Rashad Ghunaim*).

WHO Are Eligible to Receive ZAKAT?

The holy Qur'an describes how *Zakat* should be distributed.

'*As-Sadaqat* (here it means obligatory charity, i.e. *Zakat*) are only for the *Fuqara'* (the poor who do not beg), and the *Masakin* (the poor who beg) and those employed to collect the (*Zakat*); and to attract the hearts of those who have been inclined (towards Islam); and to free the captives; and for those in debt; and for Allah's cause (i.e. for *Mujahidun* - those fighting in a battle on behalf of Islam), and for the way-farer (who runs out of money); a duty imposed by Allah. And Allah is All-Knowing, All-Wise." (*Q.9: 60*)

In the light of this *Ayah* eight categories of people are eligible to receive *Zakat*, they are:

- **The *Faqir*** (destitute):

The poor who possesses half of his minimum needs or less. They are more needy than the *Miskin*.

- **The *Miskin*:**

Are poor, but are better off than the *Faqir*, like one who possesses 70% or 80% of his needs, for instance.

The *Miskin* and *Faqir* should be given of the *Zakat* that will suffice them for the coming year since *Zakat* is only due once a year, so it is only fitting that they get enough to last them until its next distribution.

The necessity should be decided on the basis of the requirement of the poor and his family's need of food, clothing, housing, and anything which one cannot do without, living on a moderate level, neither extravagantly nor very tight. (The family includes everyone whom the recipient has a responsibility to support). The level of necessity may vary from era to era and place to place and to some extent between one individual and another. What is sufficient for a person in one society is not sufficient for a person in another. And what was enough ten years ago may not be enough today. Likewise what is enough for one person may not be enough for another, according to the different number of dependents and obligatory expenditures he may have, etc.

Some religious scholars are of the opinion that necessity includes medical treatment of the ill, and helping single people to get married, and acquiring necessary books of religious knowledge.

For the *Faqir* and *Miskin* to be eligible for receiving *Zakat*, they must be Muslim and not from the lineage of Bani Hashim and their slaves. Also, they should not be close relatives of the donor. Finally, a recipient of *Zakat* should not be able-bodied who is in a situation to earn a living. The Messenger of Allah said:

"There is no portion in it for the wealthy nor for the strong, who can earn his living." *(Ahmad).*

- **The collectors of *Zakat*:**

They are those appointed by the Muslim state to perform one of the duties necessary for the establishment of *Zakat* in the society, such as collecting it, keeping its records and accounts, guarding it, transporting it and distributing it, etc.

The *Zakat* employee is eligible to be paid a wage comparable to that of a person doing a similar job in some other organization, and according to how much time he works for the *Zakat* purpose, even if he is rich, as long as he is a rational, adult Muslim, trustworthy, and qualified for the job. However, if he is from Bani Hashim he cannot receive a wage from the *Zakat* money. This is based on the *Hadith* of *Muslim*, on the authority of Al-Muttalib ibn Rabi'ah that the Prophet (peace & blessings of Allah be with him) said:

"Sadaqah (charity) is not befitting for the family of Muhammad."

- **The weak in Faith:**

These may be persons of authority and influence among their clans, tribes, nations, etc., who it is hoped, will accept Islam as their faith; or they may be shaky new Muslims whose allegiance to Islam needs to be fortified so that their belief can take root firmly; or that their peers may become Muslim, or to protect the Muslims or to avert the harm they are capable of inflicting.

This category is still eligible for *Zakat*, and it has not been abrogated. They are to be given what it takes to reconcile their hearts to Islam, and supporting and defending it. This portion may even be given to a disbeliever, because the Prophet gave Safwan ibn Umayyah a portion of the spoils of Hunayn. *(Muslim)*.

It may also be given to a Muslim, for the Prophet (peace & blessings of Allah be with him) gave to Abu Sufyan ibn Harb, Aqra' ibn Habis, and 'Uyainah ibn Hisn one hundred camels each. *(Muslim)*

- **To buy freedom of captives or slaves:**

This includes freeing a slave outright, or helping a slave who has contracted with his owner to purchase his own freedom, to make his payments. It also includes paying the ransom of Muslim prisoners of war to rescue them from the enemy.

- **Debtors:**

They are the ones who may have incurred debts and may be unable to pay them. Debts are of two kinds:

Debts incurred by a person for something which is permissible in Islam, for instance, for clothing, or his family's living expenses, or to get married, or for medical treatment, or to build a house, or necessary furnishing, or to pay for accidental damages to another person's property. In such cases he should be given what it takes to discharge the debt if he is too poor to do so himself, and the debt was incurred in obedience to Allah or in a lawful matter.

And it is required that the recipient be a Muslim, and that he should not be well-off, able to discharge the debt on his own, and that the debt was not incurred in disobedience to Allah. It is also required that the payment is already due, or will be due in the coming year, and finally, the debt must be owed to a human being, which excludes financial debts to Allah such as expiation for broken oaths or other sins or *Zakat* payments.

Debts incurred by a person for someone else's benefit, for instance, to make peace between two parties. Such a person is eligible for *Zakat*, based on the *Hadith* of Qabisah Hilali who said:

I took upon myself responsibility for someone else's debt, so I came to the Prophet (peace & blessings of Allah be with him) to ask his help. He said: "Wait until some *Zakat* payment comes in and I will arrange some of it to be given to you." Then he said, "O Qabisah, asking for money is only permissible in three cases: A man who took responsibility for another's debt, so it is permissible for him to ask until he gets what covers the debt, then he stops asking; or a man who was beset by a disaster that destroyed his property and wealth, in which case it is permissible for him to ask until he gets what it takes to put him back on his feet (or he said: what it takes to fulfill his need); or a person beset by poverty, and three men of discernment from his people say: so-and-so is poverty stricken. So asking is permissible for him until he gets what is takes to put him back on his feet, (or he said: what it takes to fulfill his need); anything besides that is corruption. O Qabisah! The one who gets it is consuming corruption." *(Muslim)*

It is also permissible to pay the debt of a dead person from *Zakat* funds, because it is not necessary for the money to pass through the debtor's hands.

- **In the way of Allah:**

This goes to volunteers for *Jihad* who are not on the government payroll, and those who guard the Muslim frontiers. Both the poor and the rich are eligible, and it does not include general charitable spending, otherwise there would have been no point in mentioning the other seven categories in the Qur'anic verse, since they would all be included in general charitable spending.

The broad meaning of *Jihad is* appropriate for inclusion in this category. That is, comprehensive, Islamic education, repelling the ideological onslaught of anti-Islamic forces, answering the doubts and suspicions they raise, distribution of useful Islamic books, and funding reliable and sincere Islamic workers to devote their energies full-time to the propagation of Islam and the countering of anti-Islamic missionary and atheist activities; etc. The holy Prophet is reported to have said:

"Strive against the polytheists with your wealth, your lives and your tongues." *(Abu Dawud).*

- **The wayfarer:**

This may be a person traveling from one land to another. If he does not have the means to complete his journey, he may be given from the *Zakat* what it takes him to complete his journey, as long as the reason for his travel is not disobedience to Allah. His travel should be for a purpose, which is mandatory or recommended in Islam, or at least permissible. Another condition is that he cannot find anyone to loan him the money. It is also permissible to give the *Zakat* to the wayfarer even if he has stayed a long time in some place in the course of his journey, if the reason for his delay is to secure some need within the range of possibility.

- It is not necessary to distribute the *Zakat* on all eight categories every year. But it is preferable bearing in mind the overall needs and benefits, as perceived by the Muslim state, or the individual who is paying the *Zakat* (in the absence of an organized collection and distribution system).

PAYING *ZAKAT* brings Great REWARDS

- To pay *Zakat* honestly and regularly is to comply with the commandments of Allah and His Messenger and seeking pleasure of Allah and His Messenger rather than being selfish for wealth.

- Multiplying the reward of one's good deeds.

The holy Qur'an states:

"The likeness of those who spend their wealth in the way of Allah, is as the likeness of a grain (of corn); *it grows seven ears, and each ear has a hundred grains. Allah gives manifold increase to whom He pleases."* (Q.2: 261).

- Giving in charity and paying *Zakat is* a proof for one's belief, and a marker indicating its presence. The Apostle of Allah (peace & blessings of Allah be with him) said: Charity is a proof. *(Muslim)*.

- Purification from the pollution of sins and degraded character. The Holy Qur'an proclaims:

"Take Sadaqah (alms) from their wealth in order to purify them and sanctify them with it..." (Q.9: 103)

- Payment of *Zakat* results in the increase of wealth. The wealth of such a person is blessed and is protected from harm.

The Apostle of Allah (peace & blessings of Allah be with him) said: Wealth never decreases due to charity. *(Muslim)*

And the Qur'an proclaims:

"...and whatsoever you spend of anything (in Allah's cause), He will replace it. And He is the Best of providers." (Q.34:39)

The giver of charity will be in the shade of his charity on the Day of Judgment. Such a person will be amongst the seven categories of the people who shall be blessed with His Shade on the Day when there will be no shade except His Shade:

- *Zakat* is also a means for seeking the Mercy of Allah:

"...and My Mercy embraces all things. That (Mercy) I shall ordain for those who are Muttaqun and give Zakat..." (Q.7: 156).

PAINFUL TORMENT is the REWARD of THOSE who do not Pay ZAKAT

Allah Most High warns those, who withhold *Zakat*. Says the Holy Book:

"...And those who hoard up gold and silver (Al-Kanz: the money, gold and silver etc., the Zakat of which has not been paid), and spend it not in the way of Allah, - announce unto them a painful torment. On the Day when that will be heated in the fire of Hell

and with it will be branded upon their foreheads, their flanks, and their backs (and it will be said unto them): 'This is the treasure which you hoarded for yourselves. Now taste of what you used to hoard.'" (Q. 9:34-35)

The Apostle of Allah (peace & blessings of Allah be with him) reportedly said:

"There is none who possessed and stored wealth without paying its *Zakat* except that it (the wealth) will be heated in the fire of Hell, then shaped into sheets with which his flanks and his forehead will be branded until Allah judges between His slaves on a day whose length will be fifty thousand years. Then he will be shown his path, either to Paradise or to the Hell-fire." (*Bukhari*)

Bukhari has recorded that the Messenger of Allah (peace & blessings of Allah be with him) said:

"Whoever is made wealthy by Allah, and does not pay the *Zakat* on his wealth, then on the Day of Judgment his wealth will be made to appear in the form of a poisonous snake with two (black) spots (over the eyes). It will coil around his neck, then it will seize him by the corners of his mouth, saying, 'I am your wealth, I am your treasure.'" Then he recited this verse:

"*And let not those, who covetously withhold of that which Allah has bestowed on them of His Bounty (wealth), think that it is good for them [and so they do not pay the obligatory charity (Zakat)]. Nay, it will be worse for them; the things which they covetously withheld shall be tied to their necks like a collar on the Day of Resurrection...*" (Q.3: 180)

The holy Prophet (peace & blessings of Allah be with him) also said:

"There is no owner of camels or cows or goats or sheep *who* does not pay their *Zakat* except that they (the animals) will come on the Day of Judgment as big and fat as they ever got, goring him with their horns, and trampling him with their hooves. As soon as the last of them has finished, the first of them will be back again, and so on until Judgment between the people is completed." *(Muslim)*

ESSENTIALS of ZAKAT

- The property on which *Zakat* applies should be fully owned, without being bound to the rights of others. The owner should have the freedom to dispose it off as he chooses. No *Zakat* applies to *Waqf* property, mortgaged property, property under legal administration or the one whose ownership is unsettled.

- On a property below the minimum prescribed under *Zakat* Rules, no dues of *Zakat* apply. The profit on which Zakat becomes due should exceed the basic needs and debt if any, of its owner. Hence no *Zakat* is to be paid on the property enough only to meet the expenses of its owner and of those dependent on him.

- *Zakat* on movable property becomes due once every year, and *Zakat* on agricultural produce be paid every time the earth yields its produce.

- For the purpose of *Zakat* there is no difference between a male or female, a prisoner or a free person. Legal guardians or trustees should pay *Zakat* on the property of infants and insane people.

- No *Zakat* is due on property such as the property of houses; private clothing, house furniture, animals used for riding, vehicles for personal use; arms, rarities, Jewelry, precious diamonds or machinery employed in industry, agriculture or in producing books. However, if any of these are used as an item of trade, then *Zakat* becomes due.

- *Zakat* is applicable to the value of business transaction. The condition is that a year should pass on the possession of the value of the deal, not of the goods. *Zakat* is applicable on the capital as well as the profits and commercial deals are to be evaluated according to the current price.

Shaikh Mohammad Abu Zahra opines that *Zakat* is due on residences or buildings used for the purpose of obtaining a profit or income.

Thus *Zakat* is applicable to the revenues of all rented buildings set for habitation or similar needs. If the building, however, gives no revenues for a period of time, *Zakat* is not applicable for that period. *Zakat* on such residences take effect the time the revenues are collected and the *Zakat* due is 1.4%.

Shaikh Mohammad Abu Zahra applies the same principle to industrial machinery — not articles used to meet the personal needs of the workers — set at factories to manufacture products. *Zakat* applies to these products every year, so that if there is profit, the poor have a right in it. *Zakat* percentage on these is 1.4%

- Zakat on amber or ambergris, pearls or fishes that are extracted from the sea should be calculated to be a fifth of their value, that is 20% of their value. The draft law of *Zakat* in Egypt fixed this condition.

- Scholars of *Fiqh* also explain that a donor of *Zakat* should not necessarily contribute indiscriminately; he may choose one or two and should ideally give priority to socially more urgent cases, and then to the less urgent ones. A donor may offer all *Zakat* to one of the eight categories, and it is not mandatory to distribute it on every category even if they are present.

- It is permissible to pay the total debt of a debtor or to pay just part of the debt.

- *Zakat* should not be paid to a disbeliever nor to an apostate (except for those whose hearts are to be drawn close); nor to one who has abandoned *Salat*, if one accepts the view that such a person has become a disbeliever except if it is given to him on the condition that he performs *Salat*, as an incentive for him.

- It is not permissible to give *Zakat* to a wealthy person, since the Prophet (peace & blessings of Allah be with him) said:

"There is no portion in it for the wealthy nor the strong (physically healthy) person who can earn (his living)." *(Abu Dawud)*

- It is not permitted for an individual to give *Zakat* to those he is obligated to support as parents, children and wives.

- It is permitted for a woman to pay her *Zakat* to her husband, if he is poor, since it is established that the wife of Abdullah ibn Mas'ud wanted to pay *Zakat* to her husband and the Prophet (peace & blessings of Allah be with him) accepted her wish.

- *Zakat* may not be transferred from one country to another except in case of pressing need such as famine, or poor people are not to be found in the country transferring the *Zakat*, or to support *Mujahidin*, or the righteous authority transfers it for general benefit, etc.

- A person from one country who gains wealth in another land, on which he is required to pay *Zakat*, must pay it where the wealth was acquired, and should not transfer it to his country of origin except in case of pressing need.

- It is permissible to give a poor person from the *Zakat* what will suffice him for several months or for the full year.

- *Zakat* is mandatory on silver and gold, whether in the form of coins, or bars, or jewellery, which is owned or lent out, or other forms, because the evidence mandating *Zakat* on gold and silver are general, without detailed distinctions. There are scholars who make an exception for jewellery which is worn or lent, that no *Zakat* is due on that, but the first point of view is stronger from the aspect of its supporting evidence and is safer in discharging ones responsibility.

- There is no *Zakat* on the property that the person needs to use: for instance, food, drink, furnishing, a house, animals, a car, clothing etc. The exception to this general rule is gold and silver jewellery.

- Property, which is set aside for rental purposes, such as real estate and cars, etc. The *Zakat* due on it is levied on the rent earned from it. After the lapse of a year, if it reaches the minimum *Nisab* by itself or in conjunction with other property in the same category, *Zakat* is due on it.

Abu Zarr related that some of the companions of the Messenger of Allah (peace & blessings of Allah be with him) asked him: O Apostle of Allah! The wealthy people have all the rewards. They offer prayer as we do, they fast as we fast, and they give charity from their wealth. The holy prophet replied: Have you not been given the means to give charity? Every time you say: 'Glory be to Allah' it is a charity; every time you say 'Allah is Great' it is a charity; every time you say' All thanks be to Allah', it is a charity; and every time you say 'There is no deity but Allah' it is a charity. And enjoining others to do good is a charity and prohibition of evil is a charity, and a man's intimacy with his wife is a charity. (*Sahih Muslim*).

Muslim has reported a Tradition on the authority of Adi Ibn Hatim who quoted the Messenger of Allah (peace & blessings of Allah be with him) as having said:

"Hour will not come until a person will seek to give in charity and will not find anyone to accept it. And each one of you will stand before Allah and there will be neither curtain nor an interpreter between him and Allah, and Allah will ask: Did I not give you wealth? He will answer: 'yes' and Allah will ask: Did I not send a Messenger to you? And again he will answer 'yes'. Then he will look to his right and he will see nothing but the fire, and then he will look to his left and will see nothing but the fire. And you should all save yourselves from the fire (of Hell) by giving even half a date in charity. And if you do not have even half a date then be charitable by saying a kind word to someone' (*Sahih Muslim*).

HAJJ
(The Annual Pilgrimage to The Holy Ka'ba)

HAJJ
The Annual Pilgrimage to the Holy Ka'ba

Allah enjoins on Muslims to pilgrimage to Ka'ba: pilgrimage thereto is duty men owe to Allah those who can afford the journey, but if any deny faith, Allah standeth not in need of any of His creatures. (Q. 11:97)

Hajj, that is, pilgrimage to the holy Ka'ba in Makkah constitutes the fifth and last of the acts of worship prescribed by Islam. It is obligatory once in a lifetime for those Muslims who are sane, of age and able to undertake the journey to Makkah. By capacity to undertake the journey, is meant that the person should have enough money to support him and his family during the absence from home. He has to be physically fit, and his way to the holy land in Arabia be safe from the dangers of war, civil strife and infectious diseases.

Hajj constitutes a form of worship for a believer with the totality of his being: with his body, mind and soul, with his time, possession and the temporary sacrifice of all ordinary comforts, convenience and tokens of status and individuality; which human beings normally enjoy, to assume for a few days condition of a pilgrim totally at Allah's service and disposal; His slave who seeks only His pleasure.

Hajj takes place during the first days of the lunar month of *Dhul-Hijjah* and ends on the ninth day of the month. The rites of Hajj center on complete submission and devotion to Allah. At the same time they commemorate an example of such total submission and obedience that prophet Ibrahim set especially in his willingness to sacrifice what he loved most in the world — his son, Ismail — at Allah's command. (Q. 37:99-113)

> *Allah enjoins on Muslims to pilgrimage to Ka'ba: pilgrimage thereto is duty men owe to Allah those who can afford the journey, but if any deny faith, Allah standeth not in need of any of His creatures. (Q. 11:97)*

The first part of the verse requires pilgrimage to be made to the sacred House of Allah by those capable of undertaking the journey, and in the second part there is severe blame on those who refrain from the performance of pilgrimage.

The pilgrimage is made to the sacred House — Ka'ba — (or the Ancient House), which dates back to the time of prophet Ibrahim (peace be upon him). Prophet Ibrahim migrated from Syria and settled down here with his wife Hajira (Hagar) and his son Ismail. And according to the Qur'an he said:

> *'O our Lord! I have made some of my offspring to dwell in a valley without cultivation, by the sacred House, in order, O our Lord! That they may establish regular prayer; so fill the heart of some among men with love towards them, and feed them with fruits, so that they may offer thanks (Q. 14: 37).*

Allah commanded Hadrat Ibrahim (peace be upon him) to erect a house of prayer in the sacred place, about which people could gather to worship Allah, glorify His Name, and express gratitude for His blessings and mercies.

The holy Qur'an reads: *And remember Ibrahim and Ismail raised the foundation of the House* (with this prayer):

> *Our Lord! Accept* (this service) *from us, for Thou art the*

All-Hearing, the All-knowing. Our Lord! Make of us Muslims, bowing to Thy (will), and of our progeny a people Muslims, bowing to Thy (will) and show us our places for the celebration of (due) rites; and turn unto us (in Mercy), for Thou art the Oft-Returning, Most Merciful (Q. 2: 127-128).

Hence Prophets Ibrahim and Ismail raised the foundations of the sacred House only after Allah had informed Ibrahim of its place. Allah says in the Qur'an:

Behold; we gave the site to Ibrahim of the House (saying): Associate not anything (in worship) with Me, and sanctify My House for those who compass it around, or stand up, or bow, or prostrate themselves (therein in prayer) (Q. 22: 26).

The obligation of pilgrimage to Allah's sacred House hence goes back to the time of Prophet Ibrahim.

While building the House, prophet Ibrahim asked his son Ismail to find a stone to be fixed as a sign, from which people may start their circumambulation. Ismail found a special, distinguished kind of stone. According to the holy Prophet Muhammad (peace & blessings of Allah be with him):

The Black Stone came down from paradise whiter than milk, but the sins of Adam's offspring turned it black.

The holy Prophet (peace & blessings of Allah be with him) kissed it while circling the House, perhaps because it was a trace from paradise, and it was carried by the hands of Ibrahim, the grand father of Prophets, and of Ismail, the father of Arabs. Special reverence and veneration is shown towards the Black Stone (*Hajar al-Aswad*) by the Muslims ever since.

Hajj and *Umrah* (the lesser pilgrimage) are obligatory on all Muslims who can afford it and are in a position to do so. Hadrat Ali reportedly said: Anyone who could have afforded to make the pilgrimage but failed to do so, and then it would not matter if he (or she) dies as a Jew or a Christian.

Ibn Abbas reported that the Messenger of Allah said: Hasten the pilgrimage for no one knows what will happen to him. (*Ahmad*)

Imam Ahmad and Ibn Majjah have reported that Hadrat Ayesha asked the prophet (peace & blessings of Allah be with him) if *Jihad* was ordained on women.

The Messenger of Allah (peace & blessings of Allah be with him) reportedly said:

Imposed on them is a *Jihad* in which there is no fighting — *Al Hajj* and *Umrah*. *Hajj* and *Umrah* are obligatory only once in a life – time.

If a Muslim intends to proceed on the pilgrimage *Hajj* or *Umrah*, he is required to advice members of his family, as well as his companions to fear Allah, obey His orders and avoid His prohibitions. He should write his debts and credits with witnesses thereon. He should also immediately embark on sincere repentance of all sins, because Allah, Most High says:

And O ye believers! Turn ye all together towards Allah in repentance that you may succeed (Q. An-Nur: 31).

The reality of repentance is to cease forthwith from committing sins, regret sincerely for those sins that one may have committed, and resolve not to return to a life of sin. Also, one should redress all wrongs he or she may have committed against people, or their property or honour. He should at least ask them to absolve him of such wrongs prior to proceeding on pilgrimage.

The Messenger of Allah (peace & blessings of Allah be with him) reportedly said: Anyone who owes a grievance or wrong to a fellow Muslim brother, be that money or honour, should absolve himself thereof immediately, before the day when there no longer will be dinars or dirhams.

In addition, the one who intends to perform *Hajj* or *Umrah* should possess enough lawful money, for the Prophet (peace

& blessings of Allah be with him) said: The Almighty Allah is good and accepts only good (deeds).

The pilgrim should not be in need of other people's money and should not ask anyone for aid or loan to pay the expences of his pilgrimage. The Prophet (peace & blessings of Allah be with him) reportedly said:

He who restrains himself and does not ask people to give him part of what they have, — Allah will make him virtuous; he who does without what the others have, — Allah will make him rich.

The pilgrim should dedicate his *Hajj* and *Umrah* for the sake of Allah and the Hereafter and for seeking nearness of Allah — in words and deeds that please Him — in those holy places. The *Hajj* should not be undertaken for the sake of the vanities of this world, or for the sake of hypocrisy, fame or boasting thereof. These are the worst of intentions; they are bound to nullify the rewards of pilgrimage.

Allah says:

> *Those who desire the life of the present and its glitter, — to them we shall pay* (the price of) *their deeds therein, — without diminution. They are those for whom there is nothing in the Hereafter but the Fire: vain are the designs they frame therein; and of no effect are the deeds that they do (Surah Hud: 15-16)*
>
> *And those who do* (make provisions for) *the Hereafter, and strive therefore with all due efforts, and have faith, — they are the ones whose striving will be thanked* (by Allah). *(Al-Isra'a: 18-19)*

The pilgrim should also learn what has been legislated as far as his *Hajj* and *Umrah* are concerned. He should understand these ordinances and make himself aware of what he may not know.

Just before proceeding for pilgrimage the pilgrim should

begin with the Name of Allah, should recite *Allahu Akbar* (Allah is the Greatest) three times and recite the verses of *Az-Zukhruf (13-14).*

Glory to Him who has subjected these to our (use), for we could never be able to do it. And to our Lord, surely is our return.

This may be followed by:

> O Lord! I beseech you to grant me righteousness and piety in this Journey of mine and to enable me to perform such deeds that please you! O, Lord, make easy this journey of mine and enable me to perform such deeds that please you! O, Lord, make easy this journey of ours, and shorten for us its long distance! O, Lord, you are the companion in travel and the guardian for my family. O, Lord, I seek refuge in you from hardship of travel, the gloominess of the scenery and the terrible vicissitudes in property and kin.

The pilgrim should repeatedly celebrate Allah's praises, ask for His forgiveness, supplicate to Him, and humble himself before Him. He should read the Qur'an, understand its meaning, perform congregational prayers, avoid gossip and futile conversation including lying, backbiting, calumny, and mockery of his friends and other Muslims.

Basic Rites (*Arkans*) of Pilgrimage

The first basic rite of pilgrimage is the *Ihram*, which legally means entering upon the state of pilgrimage. The *Ihram* is performed at a certain place, known as *Miqat*, beyond which the pilgrim should not proceed unless he is in this special state. The *miqat* is of two categories: chronical and local. The chronical *miqat* begins on the first of *shawwal* and extends till shortly before the day break of *youm al-Nahr* (The Feast of Sacrifice at Mina), whereas the local *Miqat* differs according to the countries the pilgrims come from. The places appointed en route to Makkah for *Ihram* are:

- Juhfa - for the pilgrims arriving from Egypt, Syria,

Lebanon and Morocco (Marakkesh). Al-Juhfah is a ruined village beyond Rabegh. Pilgrims presently begin their Ihram at Rabegh.

- Dhat Irq is the *Miqat* for people of Iraq and the East.
- Dhul Hudaifah presently known as Abyar Ali is the *Miqat* for the people coming from the direction of Madinah Al-Munawwarah.
- Yalam Lam is the *Miqat* for the pilgrims coming from the direction of Yemen. And
- Qarn Al-Manazil is the *Miqat* for the pilgrims coming from Najd.

The Messenger of Allah (peace & blessings of Allah be with him) fixed these *Miqats* for the groups of people mentioned above and for others who pass these *Miqats* on their way to *Hajj* or *Umrah*. It is the obligation of those who pass these stations to assume Ihram there. Those who intend to go to Makkah by air for the *Hajj* or *Umrah* should prepare themselves for *Ihram* by bathing, trimming, shaving etc, before boarding the plane, and when they approach the *Miqat* they must put on their clothes and garments and then utter the *"Talbiyah"* for the *Umrah* if there is sufficient time for that, but if there is no time for that, the pilgrim should utter the *Talbiyah* for *Hajj*. There is no blame either on putting on the *Ihram* and garment before boarding the plane, or before approaching the *Miqat*, but the intention to embark on the rite should not be announced until the pilgrim arrives at the *Miqat* or above it in the air.

As for those who live within the *Miqat* distance, like the people of Jaddah, Umm As-Salam, Bahrah, Ash-Shara'i, Badr and Masturah, and others, are not required to go to any of the *Miqat* stations, for each of them his or her house is the *Miqat* and *Ihram* should be assumed there for whatever is intended — *Hajj* or *Umrah*.

The pilgrim enters the state of *Ihram* by taking off his stitched clothes — shirt, trousers, suit, turban, gown etc. and puts on a seamless garment. For men this garment consists of two lengths of generally white material, one covering the body from the waist to ankle, the other thrown over the shoulder. Women pilgrims are allowed to go into *Ihram* in whatever clothes they like, but their whole body and head should be covered, except the face and the hands.

When the pilgrim arrives at the *Miqat* (*Ihram* Point) he is required without obligation to take a bath. The women pilgrims who arrive at *Miqat* in a state of menstruation or confinement after childbirth should take a bath and observe *Ihram* like other pilgrims with the exception of *Tawaf* (circumambulation) around the ka'ba, as the holy Prophet (peace & blessings of Allah be with him) had asked Hadrat Ayesha and Asma to do.

It is preferable for those who want to observe *Ihram* to trim their moustaches and nails and to shave their pubic hair and their armpits. The pilgrim should do that in such a way as to ensure that he would not need to do it again during the *Ihram* because trimming hair and nails and shaving is prohibited during *Ihram*. It is prohibited to trim the hair of the head and shave the beard or trim any part of it during these times.

After completing the bath and the washing and wearing the *Ihram* garments, the pilgrims are required to silently express their intention on the rite of *Hajj* or *Umrah*. The holy Prophet (peace & blessings of Allah be with him) said: Deeds are (measured) by intentions and each person (shall be judged) by what his intentions are. Should the intention of the pilgrim be to perform Umrah, he should say:

Labbayka Allahumma Umrah.

(O, Lord, here I come for the *Umrah*).

And if the intention is to perform the *Hajj* a pilgrim should say:

Labbayka Allahumma Hajj

(O, Lord, here I come for the Hajj)

It is better if this utterance is made immediately after settling down on your mount, car or any other form of transportation. As for prayers, *Tawaf* and other rites, the pilgrim is not required to utter his or her intention for such proclamation is utter sin. Since no such action has been reported about the Prophet (peace & blessings of Allah be with him) or his companions it is considered an innovation and heresy.

The wealth that a pilgrim spends to perform *Hajj* and *'Umrah* must be *Halal* (earned lawfully) so that Allah may accept it.

It is forbidden for a woman to travel for *Hajj* or anywhere else without *a Mahram* to accompany her [a *Mahram* is either her husband or close male relatives who are not permitted to marry her, like her father, brother, uncle, son etc. The *Mahram* has to be old enough to be able to protect her]. The Prophet (peace & blessings of Allah be with him) said:

"A woman may not travel except if *a Mahram* is with her." *(Bukhari).*

And he (peace & blessings of Allah be with him) said:

"Take from me your rites (the rituals of the *Hajj*)." *(Muslim).*

The best way to perform the *Hajj* and *'Umrah* is called *Tamattu'*, which means you perform *'Umrah* first, then come out of *Ihram* until *Hajj* starts, whereupon you put on *Ihram* again. The Prophet (peace & blessings of Allah be with him) is reported to have said:

"O family of Muhammad! Whoever performs *Hajj* amongst you should enter *Ihram* for *'Umrah* along with *Hajj*." *(Ibn Hibban).*

The RITES of 'UMRAH
(The Lesser Pilgrimage)

Ihram: Put on the clothes of *Ihram* at the *Miqat* and make the intention for *'Umrah* at one of the *Miqat* after putting on prescribed clothing (for men it is two unstitched garments, similar to a towel or sheet, one piece around the upper part and one piece wrapped around the lower part of the body). The intention here should be made verbally, as that is *Sunnah:* Recite:

Labbaik Allahumma bi Umrah

"At Your service (literally: "In response to Your call"); O Allah for *'Umrah".*

Thereafter, in a loud voice keep repeating the *Talbiyah:*

Labbaik Allahumma Labbaik

"At Your service; O Allah, at Your service."

Tawaf

When pilgrims reach Makkah, they pay their respect at the Sacred House and walk around the *Ka'bah* seven times, counterclockwise, starting from the corner of the *Hajar Al-Aswad* (the Black Stone), saying:

Bismillah wa Allahu Akbar

"In the Name of Allah, Allah is the Greatest."

Between the Yemeni corner and the corner of the Black Stone recite the following supplication:

"O our Lord, grant us good in this life and in the Hereafter and protect us from the torment of the Fire."

When the pilgrims reach the Black Stone, they repeat as before until they complete seven rounds. Then they pray two *Rak'ahs* behind the *Maqam Ibrahim*, reciting *Surah Al-Kafirun* in the first *Rak'ah*, and *Surah Al-Ikhlas* in the second. (After the prayer, it is *Sunnah* to drink Zamzam water and invoking Allah for greater knowledge and what one may like).

Thereafter the pilgrims are required to do *Sa'i*. They climb up the hill of *As-Safa* saying:

"*Verily! As-Safa and Al-Marwa* (two small hills in Makkah) *are of the signs of Allah. I start with what Allah started with* (As-Safa)."

Then face the *Qiblah* and raise your hands towards the sky, saying: *Allahu Akbar* three times without pointing; and say:

"*None has the right to be worshiped except Allah, Who is Alone without partners. The dominion belongs to Him and all praise belongs to Him alone. And He has power over all things. None has the right to be worshiped except Allah Alone. He executed His promise, and His slave was truthful, and He defeated the opponents Himself.*"

Recite these words three times, and repeat all of these words each time you reach *As-Safa* and *Al-Marwa*. Pray for anything you wish to. There is a certain part of the distance between the two hills, marked by green lines, where it is recommended for men to run. Make seven passages between the two hills (one-way is counted as one passage, so the whole *Sa'i* is 3.5 round trips).

Thereafter shave your whole head, or trim your hair; women should cut a small portion of their hair.

With that *Umrah* is completed and a pilgrim comes out from the state of *Ihram* (changing into normal clothes, and being free to do everything forbidden in the state of *Ihram*).

Umrah Outside The Months of *Hajj*

Those who arrive during the months other than the *Hajj* months, such as *Ramadhan* and *Sha'ban* should go into *Ihram* for *Umrah*, and make an intention for doing so inwardly and utter aloud:

'Labbayka Umrah' or Labbayka Allahumma Umrah', and thereafter recite the following *Talbiyah* of the Prophet:

"Labbayka! Allahumma Labbayka!

Labbayka! La Shareeka Laka! Labbayka!

Innal-Hamda wa'n-Ni'mata Laka,"

wal-Mulka! La Shareeka Laka!

Here I am, O Allah! Here I am!

Here I am.

There is none like unto Thee. Here I am.

All praise is to Thee; all wealth is Thine;

All power and domain are Thine, and

Thou hast no partner. O Allah!

Thou art the True Lord,

Here I am.

The pilgrim should repeatedly utter this *Talbiyah* and celebrate the praises of Allah until he arrives at the sacred House (Ka'ba) where the *Talbiyah* is to be interrupted and circumambulation of the Ka'ba to be done seven times and two *Rakahs* are to be prayed behind the station of Ibrahim (*Maqam I Ibraim*). Thereafter the pilgrim should proceed to As-Safa and Al-Marwa and walk rapidly seven times between As-Safa and Al-Marwa. Thereafter the pilgrim should get his head shaved or trim his hair. The *Umrah* is considered complete at this point.

Hajj & Umrah During The Period of Hajj

The pilgrims who arrive at *Miqat* during the months of *Hajj* or *shawwal* and *Dhul Qa'dah*, and the first ten days of *Dhul Hijjah* — have three options: *Hajj* alone, *Umrah* alone, or both *Hajj* and *Umrah*. The holy Prophet (peace & blessings of Allah be with him) gave his companions these options when he arrived at *Miqat* in the month of *Dhul Qi'dah* during the farewell pilgrimage.

The *Sunnah* for such pilgrims is that if they do not have a sacrificial animal, they should assume *Ihram* for the *Umrah* – circumambulate the Ka'ba, (seven times) walk fast between Safa and Marwa (seven times) trim their hair and their *Umrah* is complete in accordance with the instructions of the Messenger of Allah (peace & blessings of Allah be with him).

Those who bring sacrificed animal with them should maintain their *Ihram* until the day of sacrifice. They should assume *Ihram* for *Hajj* and *Umrah*. If the pilgrim (*Muhrim*) is uncertain that he will not be able to complete his *Arkans* (rites) of *Hajj* because of illness, or because he is afraid of an enemy. Then while assuming the state of *Ihram*, he should say:

"If anything obstructs me (from proceeding with the acts of worship), *the break of my Ihram will be where you have detained me"*.

The benefit for this condition is that if the pilgrim is exposed to anything that would prevent him from completing his or her *Hajj*, such as illness or an enemy, then the pilgrim is permitted to break the *Ihram* without any obligation at all.

Hajj of Minors

The *Hajj* of young children is considered valid. Imam Muslim recorded a tradition reported by Ibn Abbas that a woman who held a young child asked the prophet (peace & blessings of Allah be with him):

O' Messenger of Allah! Would there be *Hajj* for this boy also? The Prophet (peace & blessings of Allah be with him) replied: "Yes, and the reward will be yours". Similarly Ibn Yazid is reported by Imam Bukhari to have said that he was taken to the *Hajj* with the Prophet (peace & blessings of Allah be with him) when he was only seven years of age.

The pilgrimage of minors is valid but they are not exempted from the obligation of *Hajj* after they grow up. Ibn Abbas reported that the Messenger of Allah (peace & blessings of Allah be with him) said: Any child (underage person) who performs the *Hajj* and then reaches puberty, should perform another pilgrimage. If a child is below the age of discretion, his guardian should make the intention (*Niyya*) for *Ihram* on behalf of the child and utter the *Talbiyah* on its behalf. But children should be clean in attire and body during *Tawaf* (circumambulation) because *Tawaf* is like prayer. The guardian should perform (on behalf of the child) all acts of worship that they cannot handle themselves, such as throwing the pebbles and the like. If the child pilgrim is incapable of performing *Tawaf* and the *Sa'i* they can be carried to do that. In such cases it is better that the guardian who carries the children for *Tawaf* or the *Sa'i* should not perform his own *Tawaf* or *Sa'i* simultaneously. He should make the *Niyya* (intention) for *Tawaf* or *Sa'i* on behalf of the minors and thereafter perform his own *Tawaf* and *Sa'i* independently.

The children, who have attained the age of discretion, are enjoined to purify themselves of impurities before proceeding for *Tawaf* just like adult pilgrims do. *Ihram* on behalf of the children is not mandatory but a voluntary act.

What is Allowed & What is Forbidden?

Having made the intention for *Ihram*, the pilgrim — male and female — is not allowed to trim hair or nails or to use perfume. Nor is the male pilgrim in particular allowed to wear stitched clothes, that is, Shirts, under shirts, trousers, drawers, socks etc. Sandals and slippers are allowed. *Ihram* can be tied with a string or the like of it. The pilgrim is also required to take a bath and wash his hair.

Women pilgrims are permitted to wear such stitched clothes but not shirts, drawers, steppers, stockings and the like. But they are not allowed to wear any stitched material to cover the face or hands. The prophet (peace & blessings of Allah be with him) is reported to have said: *"A woman should not put on a veil or wear gloves"*. However, Women pilgrims are permitted to cover their faces and the palms if they are in the presence of foreigners.

Male and female pilgrims are also allowed to wash their clothes, in which they observe their *Ihram*, to clean them of any dirt. They can also change their clothes. However the clothes touched by saffron and safflower are not allowed.

In addition, the pilgrim should avoid all obscenities, wickedness and wrangling. (*Al-Baqarah: 197*)

The Messenger of Allah (peace & blessings of Allah be with him) reportedly said:

He who performs the Hajj and does not commit obscenity, wickedness or wrangling, will return home free from sins as in the state in which his mother delivered him.

Obscenity refers to sexual intercourse, dirty words or deeds. Wrangling implies disputes over falsehoods or over futile matters.

The male pilgrim is prohibited from covering his head or face with anything that touches it like hats, turbans or other head covers. But there is no blame on those who seek the shade of umbrellas or other such things.

The pilgrims are prohibited from hunting wild animals, or assisting in such hunting, or frightening these animals from their places, or entering into a contract of marriage, or doing sex, or getting engaged to women, or treating women with lust. Hadrat Uthman quoted the Messenger of Allah as having said: *The Muhrim is not permitted to marry or be married, nor is he permitted to propose marriage.*

However, if the pilgrim accidentally and unconsciously wears tailored clothes, covers his head, applies perfume, shaves head, trim hair or clip nails, due to forgetfulness or ignorance, there is no blame on him. However he should rectify whatever he can when he remembers or is reminded of the mistake.

It is prohibited to frighten or harm animals, cut or prick the trees and green plants of the sacred sanctuary. It is also prohibited to touch or remove a neglected or dropped thing unless it is picked up to inform about it or to return it.

The Messenger of Allah said:

This city (Makkah) enjoys a sanctity derived from Allah until the Day of Judgment; its trees shall not be cut, its animals shall not be molested, its fresh herbage shall not be cut and things dropped or neglected shall not be picked up except by the one who intends to inform about them or return them.

Mina and Muzdalifah are part of the sacred sanctuary, while Arafah is not.

Things to do on entering Makkah

When the pilgrim arrives at Makkah, he is required without obligation to take a bath before entering the city. When he arrives at the Sacred Mosque, the pilgrim should follow the *Sunnah* of the holy Prophet (peace & blessings of Allah be with him) by stepping in with his right foot first and reciting.

In the Name of Allah, and peace and blessings be upon His Messenger, I seek the protection of Allah, His Beneficent Face and ancient Authority, from the rejected Satan. O, Lord! Open for me the gates of Your Mercy."

The Pilgrim on reaching the *Ka'bah* should interrupt his *Talbiyah* prior to starting *Tawaf*, if he or she is performing the *Umrah* or *Tamattu* (interrupted pilgrimage). Thereafter he should proceed towards and face the Black Stone, touch it by his right hand and kiss it, if that is possible, without inconveniencing the other pilgrims.

Upon touching the Black Stone, the pilgrim should say: "*Bismillah, Wa Allahu Akbar*" (In the Name of Allah and

Allah is Greatest). But, if kissing the Black Stone is difficult, due to huge crowds, then the pilgrim should touch it with his right hand or with a stick and then he should kiss hand or stick with which he touched the stone. If touching it is difficult, then he should wave at it and say "*Allahu Akbar*".

The pilgrim's position during *Tawaf* should be such that the *Ka'bah* should be on his left hand side all the time. It is preferable if at the beginning of the *Tawaf* a pilgrim recites:

"*O, Lord! Believing in You, accepting Your Book, fulfilling my covenant with You, and following the Sunnah of Your prophet Muhammad*".

The Holy Prophet (peace & blessings of Allah be with him) is reported to have uttered these words at the beginning of *Tawaf.*

The pilgrim should circumambulate the *Ka'bah* seven times. During the first three rounds the gait of the pilgrim should be fast with short steps. The last four laps should begin from the Black stone and end there. Should a pilgrim doubt the number of laps, he should consider as correct the times he is sure about. During the *Tawaf* reciting verses from the Qur'an is ordained without obligation.

It is ordained without obligation for the pilgrim when he passes during the *Tawaf* between the Yemeni corner and the Black Stone to recite the following Qur'anic verse *(Al-Baqarah: 201)*:

"*Our Lord! Give us good in this world and in the Hereafter, and save us from the torment of fire* (of Hell). Whenever he passes the Black Stone he should touch it, kiss it and say: '*Allahu Akbar*'.

There is no blame in performing *Tawaf* beyond Zamzam and the *Maqam*, especially when the place is over crowded. The entire Mosque is open for *Tawaf*. But the *Tawaf* near the *Ka'bah* is better if it is possible to do so.

After the *Tawaf* the pilgrim should pray two *rakahs* behind the *Maqam*, if possible; otherwise at any other place inside the Grand Mosque. It is a *Sunnah* of the Prophet to recite, after the *Fatiha* in these two *Rakahs*, *Surah Al-Kafirun* and *Surah Ikhlas*.

After the two *Rakahs*, the pilgrim should proceed to the Black Stone to touch it with his right hand, if possible. Thereafter, the pilgrim should proceed to As-Safa through As-Safa Gate. He may climb As-Safa or stand near it but climbing is considered better. There, he should recite the Qur'anic verse'.

Behold! Safa and Marwa are among the symbols of Allah... (Surah Al-Baqarah: 158). It is recommended that the pilgrim should face the Qibla, praise Allah and recite:

"There is no deity save Allah! Allahu Akbar! There is no deity save Allah! There is none like unto Him! His is the dominion! All praise to Him He gives life and death! He has power over all things! There is no deity save Allah! Alone, He has truly fulfilled His promise, helped His servant, and alone He defeated the confederates!"

Thereafter the pilgrim should raise his hands for supplication. He should repeat this remembrance of Allah and the supplication three times. Then he should descend and walk toward Al-Marwa, until he reaches the First Flag-Post (green area), and thereafter walk faster until he reaches the second Flag Station of the green area. Women pilgrims are not permitted to run between the two flag-posts because that is considered to be an indecent and unbecoming act. They should walk at their normal speed.

Thereafter the pilgrim should continue to walk up to Al-Marwa, ascend it or stand near it. Ascending is considered better. At the site of Al-Marwa, the pilgrim should say and do what he said and did of As-Safa. Descending from Al-Marwa the pilgrim should walk back to As-Safa. He will thus have covered two of the ordained seven times of the *Sa'i*.

When the *Sa'i* (Run) is completed, the pilgrim must shave his head or trim the hair. Shaving the head is preferred for men. Women are required to only trim their hair up to the length of the tip of the finger, of every braid, and not more.

With this ritual the *Umrah* is completed but if the pilgrim has brought his sacrificial animal he should maintain his *Ihram* until he has completed his *Hajj* and *Umrah*.

Ihram For *Hajj* and Proceeding To Mina

On the eighth day of *Dhul-Hijjah* (the Day of *Tarwiyah*) it is ordained without obligation for those who are not in a state of *ihram* and for the residents of Makkah who wish to perform the *Hajj*, to assume the *Ihram* at the place of their residence. They are required to take bath and clean and perfume themselves upon *Ihram* for the *Hajj* in Makkah. Thereafter they are allowed to proceed to Mina before or after the declination of the sun at midday on the Day of *Tarwiyah*. They are enjoined to repeat the *Talbiyah* until they have thrown the pebbles at Aqaba.

The prayers of *Asr, Maghrib, Isha'a* and *Fajr* are to be performed at Mina. According to the *Sunnah* each prayer is to be performed in a shortened form (*Qasr*) without combining them, with the exception of the *Maghreb* and *Fajr* prayers, which cannot be shortened.

After sunrise on the Day of Arafah, the pilgrim proceeds from Mina to Arafat, and according to the Tradition of the holy Prophet (peace & blessings of Allah be with him) they should stay at Namirah until the declination of the sun at midday, if that is possible.

After the declination of the sun at midday, it is *Sunnah* for the pilgrims to listen to the sermon. Thereafter, the pilgrims pray *Dhuhr* and *Asr* prayers (shortened and combined) at the time of *Dhuhr*, under a single *Adhan* and two separate *Iqamahs*.

Supplications At Arafah

At Arafah, facing the *Qiblah* or Jabal Al-Rahmah, the pilgrims are required to celebrate the praises of Allah and to invoke and entreat Him, raising their hands during the invocation. It is preferable to recite the *Talbiyah* and verses from the Qur'an.

The Messenger of Allah (peace & blessings of Allah be with him) is reported to have said:

The best supplication is the one made on the Day of Arafah, and the best supplication that I and the prophets, who preceded me, made is:

There is no deity but Allah! There is no partner with Him! All power is His and all praise is to Him! He gives life and death! And He has power over all things!"

The prophet (peace & blessings of Allah be with him) also said that the dearest utterances to Allah are four:

- *Subhan Allah* (Glory be to Allah)
- *Al-Hamdu-Lillah* (Praise be to Allah),
- *La Ilaha Illa Allah* (there is no deity save Allah) and,
- *Allahu Akbar* (Allah is greatest).

Other celebrations of Allah and invocations to Him should be repeated at all times, especially on the Day of Arafah. Some of these are:

Glory be to Allah and all praise is due to Him! Glory be to the Almighty Allah!

There is no god save Allah! We worship none but Him! The favour is His, the bounty is His, and the good praise is to Him!

There is neither might nor power but by Allah.

O' Lord! Give us good in this world and good in the Hereafter, and save us from the torments of the Fire.

O' Lord! Make life for me full of every good; and make death a rest for me from every evil.

O, Lord, I seek refuge in Thee from concern and sadness, from incapacity and laziness, from cowardice and stinginess, from sin and debt, from surmounting debts and vanquishing men! O, Lord I seek refuge in Thee from leucoderma, madness, leprosy and all other evil diseases! O, Lord I beseech Thee for forgiveness and good health in this world and in the Hereafter! O' Lord, I beseech Thee for forgiveness and health for my religion and for my family and property! O' Lord, please conceal my indecencies, pacify my fears, and protect me from afore and aft, from my right and left, and from above!

O, Lord, I seek refuge in Thy Majesty from being swallowed up by the earth beneath me! O' Lord, please forgive my sins, my ignorance, my excesses; and all that Thou knowest better than I about me! O, Lord, please forgive my seriousness and my jesting, my errors and my intentions! O, Lord, please forgive what I have advanced and retarded, what I said in secret and in public, and all that Thou knowest better than I about me! O, Lord, Thou art the One who puts forward and the one who puts back, for Thou hast power over all things! O, Lord, I beseech Thee to grant me perseverance in obeying Thine orders and a strong will to follow Thy guidance. I beseech Thee to accept my thanks for Thy favours and good worship! I beseech Thee to grant me a sound heart and a sincere tongue! I beseech Thee to let me know the best of what Thou knowest! I seek refuge in Thee from the worst of what Thou knowest. I seek Thy forgiveness for what Thou knowest, for Thou art the knower of the unseen!

O' Lord of the prophet Muhammad (peace and blessings of Allah be with him) *please forgive my sin and remove the vexation of my heart and protect me from the misleading afflictions as long as Thou let me live!*

O, Lord, I beseech Thee for guidance, piety, chastity and abundance!

O' Lord, I beseech Thee for guidance and appropriateness!

On the Day of Arafah the pilgrim should humble himself before his Lord, the Almighty Allah, seek His mercy and forgiveness, fear His punishment and abhorrence. The holy prophet (peace & blessings of Allah be with him) is reported to have said: There is not a day on which Allah emancipates more of His servants from the Fire (of Hell) than on the Day of Arafah.

The pilgrims invoke and supplicate to Allah until the sun sets. Thereafter they proceed to Muzdalifah repeating the *Talbiyah*. It is not permissible to leave before sun set, because the Prophet waited until sunset. When they arrive at Muzdalifah, they combine the three *Rakahs* of the *Maghreb* prayer and the two *Rakahs* of the *Isha'a* prayer with one *Adhan* and two *Iqamahs*.

The pilgrims stay the night at Muzdalifah until the dawn (*Fajr*) prayer, and then they stand near the sacred monument, turn their faces towards *Qiblah* and raise their voices in celebrations of Allah's praises, invocations and supplications until the light of dawn shines forth. It is preferable to raise one's hands during these recitations. The pilgrims are not required to get to the sacred Monument or to climb it, because the Prophet (peace & blessings of Allah be with him) said: Muzdalifah is all places for standing.

After dawn when the light of the day is wide spread and before sunrise, the pilgrims proceed to Mina, reciting the *Talbiyah* throughout their walk. When they reach Muhassir, it is ordained without obligation for them to walk a little more quickly. When they reach Mina, they are supposed to interrupt the *Talbiyah* at Jamarat Al Aqaba, at which they are required to throw seven pebbles, one after the other. They should raise their hand when throwing each pebble, and recite *Allahu Akbar* (Allah is greatest). It is preferred to throw the pebbles from the bottom of the valley standing, with *ka'bah* to their left and Mina to their right, as the Prophet (peace & blessings of Allah be with him) did the same.

The pilgrims throw pebbles at the three columns representing

Satan, which have stood since ancient times in the village of Mina. These stone pillars stand at the site where Satan appeared to prophets Abraham and Ismail in remote antiquity, tempting them to disobey Allah when Prophet Ibrahim was taking his son to be sacrificed at Allah's command.

Thereafter the pilgrims can sacrifice their *"Hadi"* by reciting *"Bismillah' Wallahu Akbar!* This is from you and it goes to you," and face the *Qiblah*. The *Sunnah* is to slaughter a camel while it is standing with its leg fettered and to slaughter a cow or a sheep while it is lying on its left side. It is preferred that the pilgrim eats some of the *"Hadi"*, give some as present, some as alms. The Qur'an says: *Then eat ye thereof, and feed the distressed ones in want. (al-Hajj: 28).*

The slaughter time continues until sunset on the third day of *Tashreeq*. The period of slaughtering consists of that day and three days thereafter.

After the sacrifice, the pilgrim should shave his head or trim his hair, but shaving is better, as the Prophet invoked Allah's mercy and forgiveness three times for those who shave their head, but only once for those who trim their hair. It is not enough to trim the hair of some parts of the heads, but all parts should be trimmed, just like shaving. Women are required to trim at most the length of the finger's tip from every braid.

After leaving Jamrat Al-Aqaba and shaving the head or trimming the hair of men, all the prohibitions of *Ihram* are lifted, but sex is not allowed. This *"Tahallul"* (break of the *Ihram*) is called the first *"Tahallul"* after which it is the *Sunnah* for the pilgrim to use perfumes and proceed to Makkah for *Tawaf Al-Ifadah* (essential circumambulation).

Tawaf Al-Ifadah and *Tawaf Al-Ziyarah* is a *"Ruku"* pillar of *Hajj*, without which the pilgrimage would not be complete. This is mentioned in the Qur'anic Verse Al-Hajj: 29:

Then let them complete the rites prescribed for them, fulfill their vows, and (again) *circumambulate the Ancient House.*

It is recommended that thereafter the pilgrim should drink water from the well of Zamzam and to make supplications as Abu Zarr reports that the holy Prophet (peace & blessings of Allah be with him) said about Zamzam's water:

'It is a savoury food'. According to Abu Dawud the Messenger of Allah also said: (Zamzam water) is a cure for sicknesses.

After *Tawaf Al-Ifadah* the pilgrims return to Mina where they spend three days, including the nights, and throw stones at the three *Jamarat* after the declination of the sun at midday on each of the three days. But if anyone wants to leave in two days, there is no blame on him (or her).

Enjoining the Good and Forbidding the Evil

Among the most important things that a pilgrim must do is to enjoin what is right and forbid what is evil, and to perform the obligatory five prayers in congregation. All pilgrims to the House of Allah should avoid all that has been prohibited by Allah such as adultery, homosexuality, stealing, usury, cheating in transactions, betrayal of trust, drinking of intoxicants, smoking, arrogance, covetousness, hypocrisy, backbiting, calumny, mockery of Muslims, amusements such as discs, lutes, rababs, flutes, and the like, listening to songs and musical instrument on the radio, and other media, chess, gambling, etc. No obscenity and transgression is allowed during the *Hajj* period.

Also prohibited are invoking the dead, seeking their assistance, offering sacrifices in their name, or swearing by anyone other than Allah. The Messenger of Allah (peace & blessings of Allah be with him) is reported to have said: He who swears by anyone but Allah has rejected the faith or associated partners with Him.

The pilgrims are required to do good deeds throughout their stay in Makkah and Madinah — to offer prayers and *Tawaf* around the sacred House, invoke Allah's blessings and peace upon the holy Prophet (peace & blessings of Allah be with him).

When the pilgrim wishes to leave Makkah, he should perform the farewell *Tawaf* of the House.

Visiting The Prophet's Mosque In Madinah

It is a *Sunnah* to visit the Mosque of the Prophet (peace & blessings of Allah be with him) before or after the *Hajj* for it is reported on the authority of Abu Hurayra that the Messenger of Allah (peace & blessings of Allah be with him) said: A prayer in this Mosque of mine is better than a thousand prayers in any other mosque, with the exception of the Sacred Mosque (in Makkah). Abdullah Ibn Al-Zubayr added that the Prophet (peace & blessings of Allah be with him) said:

'A prayer in the sacred Mosque (in Makkah) is better than one hundred prayers in the mosque of mine.

It is recommended that while entering the Mosque of the Prophet the visitor should step in with his right foot and recite:

In the Name of Allah, peace and blessings be upon the Messenger of Allah. I seek refuge in the Almighty Allah, His Noble Face, His ancient authority, from the Rejected Satan. O, Allah, please open for me the gates of Thy Mercy'.

Once inside the Mosque the visitor should perform two *Rakahs*, preferably at *Al-Rawdhah*, because the holy Prophet (peace & blessings of Allah be with him) said: Between my house and my *mimbar* (pulpit) is a garden (*rawdah*) of the gardens of paradise.

After offering the prayers, the visitor should visit the grave of the holy prophet (peace & blessings of Allah be with him) and his two companions - Abu Bakr and Umar (may Allah be pleased with them). He should stand by the grave of the Prophet (peace & blessings of Allah be with him) and politely recite his salutations to him saying:

Peace be upon you, O' Messenger of Allah, as well as the mercy of Allah and His blessings.

It is also recommended to recite the following at the grave of the holy Prophet (peace & blessings of Allah be with him):

Peace be upon you, O Messenger of Allah! Peace be upon you whom Allah selected as the best of His creation! Peace be upon you, O Master of all Messengers and Leader of the Righteous! I bear witness that you have proclaimed the message, delivered the trust, advised the people, and fought the best Jihad in the path of Allah.

It is also recommended to recite salutations on the graves of Abu Bakr and Umar and pray that Allah be pleased with them.

It is the *Sunnah* to perform the five obligatory prayers at the Mosque of the prophet preferably in the first row.

It is not permitted to touch or kiss the 'Hujrah' (prophet's chamber) or to circumambulate it. And it is not permitted to ask the Prophet (peace & blessings of Allah be with him) for anything. Directing such requests is tantamount to joining partners with Allah.

No one is permitted to seek the intercession of the Prophet for this is the prerogative of Allah and cannot be sought except from Him.

The Messenger of Allah (peace & blessings of Allah be with him) is reported to have said not to make his grave a place of pilgrimage. On the other hand he reportedly said:

'*Invoke Allah's blessings upon me, for your invocation reaches me wherever you are*".

Visiting the grave of the Prophet is not an obligation imposed on the Muslims, nor is it a pre-condition for an accepted pilgrimage. It is, however, a *Sunnah* to visit the Mosque of the Prophet. It is also recommended for the visitor to Madinah to visit the Mosque of Quba and to pray therein, because the Messenger of Allah used to do so. Sahl Ibn Hunayf reported the Prophet as saying: whoever purifies himself in his house and then comes to the Mosque of Quba and performs one prayer therein, will be rewarded as if he has performed the *Umrah*.

It is also a *Sunnah* to visit the graves at Al-Baqee and those of the martyrs, as well as the grave of Hadrat Hamza and invoke Allah's blessings upon the dwellers of these graves.

The prophet (peace & blessings of Allah be with him) used to recite the following at these places:

"Peace be upon you, O people of the graves. Peace be upon you, O people of the Land, O Believers and Muslims! We shall, Allah willing, follow you. We beseech the Almighty Allah to grant protection and freedom from punishment to us and to you" (Muslim).

The VIRTUES of HAJJ and 'UMRAH

Hajj is a great gathering of Muslims. It provides a unique opportunity to the great *Umma* of Islam to meet and know each other.

The holy Prophet (peace & blessings of Allah be with him) described *Hajj* as the supreme act of worship. It is a means for the believers to renew their faith in Allah. In spirit, *Hajj* combines all the other acts of worship. While other acts of worship are about remembering Allah; *Hajj* is about reaching Him. When pilgrims stand before the holy Ka'bah, It is like standing before Allah. It is not the rites of worship that are so important during *Hajj* but the spirit in which they are carried out.

The Apostle of Allah (peace & blessings of Allah be with him) said:

"From one *'Umrah* to another is expiation for what is between them (i.e. of sins) and the *Hajj Mabrur* has no reward except Paradise."

(*Hajj Mabrur* is the *Hajj* accepted by Allah for being performed perfectly according to the Prophet's *Sunnah* with legally earned money avoiding the sin and evils during *Hajj*.)

And the Apostle of Allah (peace & blessings of Allah be with him) said:

"One who performed *Hajj* and did not speak obscenely, nor acted corruptly, shall return without his sins, like the day his mother gave birth to him."

Umrah (the lesser pilgrimage) is permitted at anytime, but it has the most reward during the month of *Ramadhan*, as the Prophet (peace & blessings of Allah be with him) reportedly said: *Umrah* in Ramadhan is equal to *a Hajj* (in reward).

- One *Salat* in *Al-Masjid Al-Haram* (the Sacred Mosque in Makkah) has more reward than 100,000 *Salat* in other mosques. The holy Prophet (peace & blessings of Allah be with him) said:

"A *Salat* in this mosque of mine (i.e. in Madinah) is better than 1,000 *Salat* in any other mosque, except *Al-Masjid Al-Haram* (Ka'bah in Makkah)."

And he (peace & blessings of Allah be with him) also said:

"And one *Salat* in *Al-Masjid Al-Haram* is better than 100 *Salat* in my *Masjid*." (*Ahmad*)

The Spirit and Significance of the *Hajj*

In addition to its spiritual aspects, *Hajj* is also remarkable for the fact that it brings together from every part of the earth an immense diversity of human beings, who, in spite of vast differences of culture and language, form one community (*ummah*), all of them professing and living by the same faith and all devoted to the worship of Allah. It is a tremendously moving experience — assuredly the ultimate experience in human brotherhood.

The *Hajj* is an exercise par excellence in devoting oneself to Allah, in overcoming one's egoism and in surrendering one's whole being to Allah. As such *Hajj* is a supreme spiritual experience that has no equal. The holy Ka'bah arouses memories of prophet Abraham, the father of prophets, and his son Ismail, who erected its structure. Circling the Ka'bah is a re-enactment of the worship performed by prophets Ibrahim and Ismail (peace be upon them) and the believers who have followed their example, as well as a bridge between the early days of Islam and our own times, and of the covenant of Muslims with Allah to cling to this faith.

The Run (*Sa'i*) between Safa and Marwa commemorates the frantic running of Hadrat Hajira (Hagar), the wife of Prophet Abraham and mother of Ismail, overtaken by thirst and on the verge of death, when Allah made water gush from the earth through the well of Zamzam. The pilgrims remember the spirit of sacrifice by Prophet Ibrahim of his son Ismail by offering sacrifices at Mina, where Prophet Ibrahim attempted to sacrifice Ismail but ended up sacrificing a ram. The sacrifice of animals during *Hajj* also reflects the sincerity and gratitude of Muslims towards Allah. And down through the ages *Hajj* has continued to serve as a major unifying influence in Islam.

Likewise just as Prophet Ibrahim had thrown stones at Satan, who tried to mislead him, the pilgrims, in memory of this event, throw stones at the pillars of Jamarat. The assembly of the pilgrims on the plain of Arafah is spiritually the high point of *Hajj* where the pilgrims promise to lead their lives on truth and for the pleasure of Allah. Arafat is of special significance because it was here that the holy Prophet (peace & blessings of Allah be with him) gave a sermon that is known as the Sermon of the Farewell *Hajj*. Presently at this spot stands the Mosque of Nimra.

In 632 A.D. the holy Prophet (peace & blessings of Allah be with him) seated on a camel, delivered his last sermon to over 100,000 pilgrims. On this solemn occasion he said:

- All believers are brothers to each other
- All believers must live in peace with one another
- All mankind is children of Adam and Eve.
- Men have rights over their women as women have rights over their men.
- All must respect the rights and properties of the neighbours
- Usury is banned
- I am leaving behind me two things_ the Qur'an and the example of my life – *Sunnah*. If you follow these, you will not stray from the right path.
- Worship Allah, be steadfast in prayer, fast during *Ramadhan*, pay alms (*Zakat*) to the less fortunate, and perform *Hajj*.

JIHAD

(The All-Round Struggle in the Path of Allah)

JIHAD
The All-Round Struggle in the Path of Allah

*And fight in the way of Allah,
those who fight you,
and transgress not the limits,
verily Allah loveth not the transgressors.*

The word *Jihad* is derived from the word *Jahada* that means to exert. Literally *Jihad* means exertion, striving, but in Juridical-religious sense, it signifies the exertion of one's power, to the utmost of one's capacity, in the path of Allah.

Jihad is the last of the fundamentals of Islam. The duty of *Jihad* is laid down in the Holy Qur'an and in the Tradition of Prophet Muhammad. One who exerts himself physically and mentally or spends his or her wealth and property in the way of Allah is indeed engaged in *Jihad*.

But in the language of the *Shariah* this word is also used for war that is waged solely for the purpose that "the word of Allah shall alone prevail." However, the slightest desire for worldly gain pollutes the purity and mars the nobleness of *Jihad*. This supreme sacrifice of life in defence of the faith devolves on all Muslims. The holy Qur'an reads:

Not equal are the holders-back among the believers save those who are disabled and the strivers in the way of Allah with their riches and lives. Allah hath preferred in rank the strivers with their lives above the holders-back and unto all,

Allah hath promised good. And Allah hath preferred the strivers above holders-back with a great reward. (Q. 4: 95)

The Holy Book makes it clear that *Jihad* denotes two kinds of strivings: One should strive with the help of God-given faculties, both mental and physical; and to strive with the help of resources which one may posses.

Ibn Rushd argues that *Jihad* is an all-round struggle and makes it obligatory for a Muslim to exercise all his powers, intellectual or physical capacities, gifts of speech, or moral strength, courage and steadfastness in the face of hardship and with the help of worldly riches. *(Ibn Rushd. Vol. I, P259)*

The holy Prophet (peace & blessings of Allah be with him) explained the true qualities of a *Mujahid*, the one who strives in the path of Allah, as the one who tries to struggle against his self, that is, evil self *(Tirmidhi-Abwab Fazail al-Jihad)*.

According to Ibn Qayyim:

The *Jihad* against the enemies of Allah with one's life is only part of the struggle that a true servant of Allah carries on against his own self for the sake of his Lord. This striving against the evil tendencies that dominate his mind and heart is more important than fighting against the enemies in the outside world. It is in fact the basis on which the struggle in the path of Allah can be successfully launched. *(Zad al-Ha'ad, II: 103)*

According to Imam Raghib, a Muslim is required to fight against three foes:

- Against the visible enemy.
- Against the Devil.
- Against his self (*nafs*)

(Raghib al-Isfahani, I: 259)

Ibn Rushd maintains that the believer may fulfill this struggle in four ways — by his heart, by his tongue, by his hands, and by the sword. The first of these implies that a Muslim should develop his sensitivities to the point of excellence, so much so that nothing, which is evil, should find its way either in his heart or in his mind. He should develop aversion against evil and a strong desire to fight it tooth and nail, whether it is found within him or in the outside world.

Similarly the gift of expression is to be used for protesting against evils in human life. The Holy Qur'an elucidates the way in which the power of expression is to be used for inviting people to the path of Allah.

Invite (all) to the way of their Lord with wisdom and goodly exhortation and argue with them with that which is the best. (Q. 16:125)

The holy prophet (peace & blessings of Allah be with him) explained that *Jihad* consists not only of using the sword, but even when a Muslim uses his tongue for protesting against the atrocities of the tyrants, he is waging *Jihad*.

Ibn Majjah has noted that the Prophet (peace & blessings of Allah be with him) reportedly said: *whoever amongst you see something abominable, he should endeavour to change it with his hand, in case he has power to do it. But if he lacks the requisite power, he should than use his tongue, and if he is powerless in this also, he must than hate it from the heart of his heart, and this in fact is the weakest (state) of faith.* (Ibn Majjah, Kitab al-Fitan).

Abu Sayeed Khudri reported that the Messenger of Allah (peace & blessings of Allah be with him) said:

The best Jihad is uttering of the word of truth in the face of a tyrannical ruler.

At the same time *jihad* implies fighting in the way of Allah when the use of arms becomes a dire necessity. In the face of threats and dangers the believers are required to face aggression bravely and manfully and to participate in Just wars.

However, war in Islam is not a casual phenomenon of violence; it is one of the phases of human strivings (*Jihad*) against all that is evil, whether in thought, or feeling or action.

In fact Islam has the greatest respect not only for the lives of human beings but even for those of animals and plants. Many verses in the Holy Book speak eloquently of the sanctity of life:

> *And there is not an animal on the earth, nor a bird that flieth with its two wings, but are communities like unto you, Nothing have we omitted from the Book, then they (all) shall be gathered to their Lord in the end. (Q. 6: 38)*

The holy Prophet (peace & blessings of Allah be with him) repeatedly emphasized the fact that not only the life of man, even the life of a small bird is extremely precious and cannot be taken without sufficient reason.

> *Whoever kills the swallow, or even a more insignificant bird than that, without any reason, shall be answerable to Allah for the slaughter.*

On another occasion the Messenger of Allah (peace & blessings of Allah be with him) warned those who maltreated the animals:

> *If Allah in His infinite mercy pardons the ill treatment, which is meted out to animals, at your hands; it means not that you have been relieved of the heavy burden of sins. (Musnad, Ahmad Ibn Hanbal VI: 44)*

Human life is given a still greater security and no one is permitted to violate the sanctity of human life, without sufficient reason.

> *Those who invoke not, with Allah, any other deity, nor slay such life as Allah has made sacred except for just cause. (Q. 25:68)*

Human life is sacred to the extent so far as its activities are confined to reasonable limits, but justice demands that tyranny and oppression should not be allowed to create havoc in the world. All civilized societies use violence in the interest of peace and prosperity and to contain aggression and terror against the peaceful and innocent.

That is why the Qur'an says:

> *Permitted are those who are fought against, because they have been oppressed, and verily to (provide) succour (for) them Allah is potent.* And
>
> *Those who have been unjustly driven forth from their abodes merely because they say: 'our Lord is Allah! ... Verily Allah is strong, Mighty.*

The Qur'an explains the function of war as a moral necessity and exhorts the believers to actively take part in it.

> *And what aileth thee that ye fight not in the way of Allah, and for the oppressed among men and women and children who say: our Lord! Take us forth from the town whereof the people are wrongdoing, and appoint (for) us from before Thee a patron and appoint (for) us from Thee a helper (Q. 4:75)*

It is significant that the war that is waged for upholding the cause of the oppressed is named by the holy Qur'an as "fight in the way of Allah". At the same time the holy Book makes a clear distinction between the war that is fought for the sake of Allah and the war that is waged in the cause of evil.

> *'Those who believe fight in the way of Allah and those who disbelieve fight in the way of Satan; verily feeble indeed is the cunning of the devil. (Q. 4: 70)*

Clearly, then, those who wage war for self-glorification, self-aggrandizement, or for the exploitation of the weaker people, are indeed the friends of the devil. Conversely those who take up arms to curb tyranny and oppression and to eradicate evil, are the ones who fight in the way of Allah.

It is narrated on the authority of Abu Musa al-Ash'ari that once a man visited the holy prophet (peace & blessings of Allah be with him) and asked: A person fights for booty, another fights for fame and another raises arms to prove his courage and bravery — who among these should be considered a fighter for the sake of Allah? The Messenger of Allah (peace & blessings of Allah be with him) remarked:

He who raises his arms with the sole objective that the word of Allah should become supreme is the one who fights for the cause of Allah. (*Bukhari, Kitabal-Jihad wa al-Siyar III: 139*)

Thus every war is not sanctified as *Jihad* in Islam. And it is not feasible to assert with certainty whether a man killed in warfare is a martyr or not; since martyrdom of a person depends upon the intention with which he participates in the battle. Allah, alone, is the rightful Judge in this matter. The holy Prophet (peace & blessings of Allah be with him) is reported to have remarked:

Allah knows fully well who strives in His cause and sustains injury for His sake. (*Bukhari*)

Thus *Jihad* is not an act of aggression for the sake of material interests or a wanton display of national or tribal power, but it is a sacred duty assigned to every Muslim in the interests of humanity, peace and justice. These noble ends are described as 'fighting in the way of Allah.'

But waging war in the way of Allah is regulated in such a way that it ceases to be a sheer drive for power.

And fight in the way of Allah, those who fight you, and transgress not the limits, verily Allah loveth not the transgressors.

The holy prophet (peace & blessings of Allah be with him) clearly set the limits that should not be transgressed by those engaged in the holy war. The non-combatants, (who do not or cannot take part in actual fighting) women and children, the aged and the infirm, the blind, the imbeciles, the travellers and those devoted to monastic services are not to be harmed at all.

On one occasion the holy Prophet (peace & blessings of Allah be with him) is reported to have warned:

Do not kill the old verging on death, nor children and babies or the women. Do not steal anything from the booty and collect together all those things, which fall to your lot in the battlefield and do good. Allah loves those who do good (Abu Dawood).

The Messenger of Allah (peace & blessings of Allah be with him) forbade wanton destruction of the crops and property of the enemy either at the time of invasion or at the time of conquest.

The holy war in Islam, therefore, is not the wild expression of the baser elements of man, but a sacred struggle to achieve certain definite noble ends.

Abu Sayeed Al-Khudri reported that the Messenger of Allah (peace & blessings of Allah be with him) said:

> There is a deed which will elevate anyone one hundred degrees in Paradise, and elevation of one degree to the other is equal to the distance between heaven and earth.

Abu Sayeed asked: what is that deed?

The prophet (peace & blessings of Allah be with him) replied: To strive in the cause of Allah, to strive in the cause of Allah.

It was related by Abu Hurayra that the Messenger of Allah (peace & blessings of Allah be with him) said:

> Whoever dies and did not strive in the cause of Allah and did not intend to do so, then he would have died having a trait of hypocrisy. (Sahih Muslim)

Salman reported that he heard the Apostle of Allah (peace & blessings of Allah be with him) say:

> Striving one day and night in the cause of Allah is better than fasting and praying for a whole month. And if (such a person) dies, his deeds will continue to be rewarded, and he will be spared from the chastisement of the grave.

Anas ibn Malik reported that the Messenger of Allah (peace & blessings of Allah be with him) said:

Going to and fro in the cause of Allah is much better than the life of this world and all that is in it.

Sahl ibn Hunaif related that the Apostle of Allah (peace & blessings of Allah be with him) said:

Whoever asks Allah sincerely for martyrdom; Allah will make him dwell in the abode of the martyrs, even if he dies upon his couch.

Amr ibn Al-A'as reported that the prophet (peace & blessings of Allah be with him) said:

A martyr is forgiven all his sins except debt.

Jihad essentially means to stand up in opposition to despotism and injustice (Q.4: 75) and on behalf of the oppressed. As resistance to injustice it has the potential of being used to mobilize political and social struggles for the achievement of economic, political and social justice as well as for realizing the essential Islamic values of justice, benevolence, humanism and universalism. The holy Qur'an emphasizes the principle of justice (*adl*) benevolence (*Ihsan*) compassion (*Rahmah*) and wisdom (*hikmah*). However the greater *Jihad*, as explained by the holy Prophet (peace & blessings of Allah be with him) involves the effort of each Muslim to struggle to improve oneself, to strive to become a better human being.

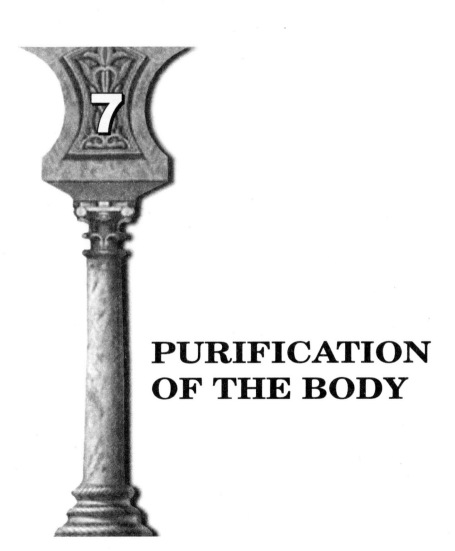

PURIFICATION OF THE BODY

PURIFICATION OF THE BODY

Cleanliness is half the Faith *(Prophet Muhammad)*

Purification and cleanliness is the foundation on which other Islamic practices are based. In the holy Qur'an and the *Sunnah* of the Prophet (peace & blessings of Allah be with him) great emphasis is laid on cleanliness. The Messenger of Allah (peace & blessings of Allah be with him) described cleanliness as half of the faith.

The holy Qur'an says:

Allah loves those who make themselves pure. (Q.9:108).

The Apostle of Allah (peace & blessings of Allah be with him) emhasised cleanliness as a necessary preliminary to the worship and adoration of Allah. At the same time he made it clear that mere external, or rather physical, purity does not imply true devotion. He distinctly laid down that the Almighty can only be aproached in purity and humility of spirit. The holy prophet (peace & blessings of Allah be with him) declared the most important purification to be the cleaning of the heart from all blameworthy inclinations and frailties and the mind from all vicious ideas and from all thoughts which distract attention from Allah. The Messenger of Allah cautioned all Muslims to ensure that their bodies be clean and free from impurity, and the place of worship be clean. The idea is to make every believer habitually clean at all times. The holy Prohet (peace & blessings of Allah be with him) is reported to have remarked: ***Cleanliness is next to godliness.***

The holy Qur'an says that the purpose of the commands regarding cleanliness and purity before every prayer by having a bath or by performing ablution (*Wudhu*) and to keep the attire and place of worship clean is the desire of Allah to keep you pure for which you should be grateful to Allah.

> *Allah does not wish to place you in difficulty, but to make you clean and complete the favour to you that you may be grateful (Q. 5:6)*

The Messenger of Allah (peace & blessings of Allah be with hium) was not only fastidious about cleanliness but also demonstrated to his followers the supreme pattern of cleanliness and purity so as to teach them and guide them in this matter. It is reported in many authentic Traditions that whenever the Prophet woke up from sleep his first act was to clean his teeth by using *Miswak* (toothstick/ dentifrice) and he used to do so before every prayer. And according to a Tradition related by Hadrat Ayesha the Prophet would always clean his teeth whenever he returned home from outside and the last act of his holy life was to clean his teeth by *miswak*. According to a Tradition the holy prophet (peace & blessings of Allah be with him) is reported to have said that were it not for the inconvenience caused by making cleaning of teeth mandatory before every prayer, he would have done so.

The holy Prophet (peace & blessings of Allah be with him) has been quoted by Abd Allah ibn Umar as saying:

> *Allah does not accept the prayer which is offered without purity and does not accept charity from wealth that has been stolen from booty.*

According to another Tradition, related by Abu Sayeed Khudri, purity is mentioned as the key to prayer *(Sahih Sunan, ibn Maja)*

According to a Tradition related by Abd Allah Bihiyi, the Messenger of Allah (peace & blessings of Allah be with him) is reported to have said: when a believer rinses his mouth during ablution, minor sins committed by his mouth are washed out, when he cleans his nose, minor sins committed by his nose are blotted out. When he washes his face, minor sins committed by his face are washed off, so much so that sins committed by his eyes and eyelashes too are washed off. When he washes his hands, all minor sins committed by his hands are pardoned, so much so that sins beneath the nails are also washed off. When the believer wipes his head during ablution minor sins committed by his head are forgiven including the sins of his ears. When he washes his feet minor sins committed by his feet including those committed by the nails of his feet are pardoned.

And when the believer proceeds to the mosque after completing ablution, with the intention of offering prayers, his position is elevated. *(Quoted from Nisai).*

Purity and Impurity of Water

According to the Islamic belief water in considered pure in itself and it has the capacity to purify other things. Rainwater, snow and hail water are declared to be pure as the holy Qur'an asserts:

"And we send down pure water from the Sky" (Q.25:48).

Similarly water of flowing springs and rivers and sea water are also declared to be pure. According to a Tradition related by Ahmad the holy Prophet (peace & blessings of Allah be with him) is reported to have said that sea water is purifying and its creatures are licit *(halal).*

Likewise water of Zamzam, spring of the holy Ka'ba, is considered pure.

Indeed Ahmed reports the holy Prophet (peace & blessings of Allah be with him) as saying: *water is purifying, nothing makes it impure.*

Accordingly used water, that is water which falls off the limbs when performing ablution or taking bath retains its purifying quality, just like ordinary water, based on the fact that it started out as purifying and there is no proof in the *Shariah* (Islamic Law) indicating a change in its status.

In case the pure water gets mixed up with other clean substances, for instance soap, saffron, or flour etc. it remains pure as long as the quantity of other clean substances is not large enough to alter water into something else, in which case it becomes incapable of purifying anything else.

If the taste or colour or smell of water changes due to its mixing with any filthy substance then it is forbidden to be used as a purifying agent, for ablution, bathing, cleaning etc. However if the taste, colour or smell of water does not change inspite of some filthy substance coming into contact with it, in that case it continues to be a purifying agent.

According to the *Four Sunan,* the holy Prophet (peace & blessings of Allah be with him) is reported to have said, that if the quantity of water is two Qullahs (a big water container made of the hide of an animal) it does not carry impurities.

According to a Tradition transmitted by Abu Qatada the holy Prophet (peace & blessings of Allah be with him) said that cat is not an impure animal and it is reported from Hadrat Ayesha that the Apostle of Allah used to perform ablution from water touched by a cat. Any food or drink touched by a cat is not therefore impure.

It is also related by Abu Hurayra that the holy Prophet (peace & blessings of Allah be with him) said when a fly falls into a vessel containing some drink, it should be fully dipped in it and then thrown away (and the drink can then be consumed) There is contamination in one wing of the fly and cure in another. *(Sahih Bukhari)*

Precepts Regarding Washrooms

While entering a washroom and/ or lavatory step in with your left foot; and when leaving it, step out with the right foot.

Before entering the bathroom one should recite the following lines:

In the name of Allah, O Allah! I seek refuge in You from the male and female devils.

And after leaving the toilet say:

Your forgiveness (O Lord)! (Cited by Tirmidhi)

It is prohibited not to carry anything containing the Name of Allah into the bathroom, washroom, toilet etc. unless there is risk of losing it; if it is left outside.

It is related by Anas ibn Malik that the Apostle of Allah (peace & blessings of Allah be with him), before entering the bathroom, used to remove his ring on which was inscribed: Muhammad Messenger of Allah.

It is not considered appropriate that one should defecate in the open unless it is absolutely necessary. In that event an isolated place should be preferred. It is better to be away from people and hide oneself while defecating. Avoid places where people are likely to assemble as under a shade, along the path ways etc.

One should refrain from speaking when relieving oneself.

Remember to respect the direction of the *Qiblah* (the Sacred Mosque in Makkah) by not facing it and by not keeping your backside directly towards it.

Do not urinate where you take your bath or in a still or running water.

It is forbidden to urinate in a standing position as it is likely to defile your body and clothes.

All impurities should be cleaned from private parts by the use of water, paper or with other pure things such as stones.

Using the right hand to clean private parts should be avoided as the right hand is used for eating and other clean functions. Hands should be carefully washed after cleaning the private parts. After urinating the organ should be purified by clean water.

It is reported from Abu Qatada that the holy Prophet (peace & blessings of Allah be with him) said:

when passing urine, do not touch private parts with right hand; nor wash them with the right hand.

And Abu Hurayra reported that the Apostle of Allah (peace & blessings of Allah be with him) said:

Do not answer the call of nature on the pathway or under a shady tree.

Cleanliness of Sexual Impurities

According to a Tradition recorded by Bukhari on the authority of Abu Hurayra the holy Prophet (peace & blessings of Allah be with him) reportedly said. A believer, under no circumstances is impure. Hadrat Ayesha is reported to have said that the Messenger of Allah (peace & blessings of Allah be with him) remembered Allah in every state *(Muslim)*. However Hadrat Ali is reported to have related that the holy Prophet "taught us the Qur'an in every state except in the state of sexual impurity." *(Tirmidhi)*.

The holy Prophet (peace & blessings of Allah be with him) emphasized cleanliness of body and attire following wet dreams and sexual acts. Guidance in this regard is also offered in the holy Book.

If you are in a state of Janabah (due to sexual intercourse or discharge) *purify yourself* (wash your whole body). *(Q.5:6)*

O you who believe! Approach not prayer when you are in a drunken state until you know (the meaning) *of what you utter, nor when you are in a state of Janabah except when traveling on the road* (without enough water or just passing by a mosque), *till you wash your whole body (Q.4: 43).*

According to Abu Hurayra the Messenger of Allah (peace & blessings of Allah be with him) reportedly said: when a husband has sexual intercourse with his wife, bath is obligatory although there may be no emission *(Bukhari).*

Bath is also obligatory if a man or a woman has a wet dream and when there is discharge from the sex organs. Indeed bath is obligatory when the private parts of a male and female come into contact; whether emission takes place or not. However in cases of *Mazzi*, whitish discharge, bath is not obligatory. It is sufficient to wash private parts and perform ablution (*Wudhu*).

Ablution is also recommended if a man wants to have sexual intercourse for the second time. According to a Tradition recorded by Muslim on the authority of Abu Sayeed Khudri the Apostle of Allah (peace & blessings of Allah be with him) said: when a person has sexual intercourse with his wife and he again desires to have it for the second time, he should first perform ablution (*Wudhu*).

Before taking bath for purifying sexual impurity, it is suggested that one should wash his hands to begin with. Hadrat Ayesha is reported to have narrated that the Messenger of Allah (peace & blessings of Allah be with him) used to perform ablution before proceeding to have bath to purify sexual impurity *(Muslim).*

Water does not get contaminated if a person in a state of *Janabah* dips his or his hands into it. According to a Tradition recorded by Abu Dawud on the authority of Abdullah ibn Abbas, a companion of the Prophet had a bath for purifying sexual impurities by using water fram a tub. The Messenger of Allah (peace & blessings of Allah be with him) arrived to perform ablution or bath and took water from the same tub. The companion said: O Messenger of Allah! I was sexually impure and had bath from the water of the tub. The Prophet (peace & blessings of Allah be with him) remarked that the water was not impure.

Bath is ordained to be obligatory under certain conditions. For instance if one is in a state of *Janabah* (Sexual impurity) or in a state of menstruation as in the case of women.

The holy Book says:

They ask you concerning menstruation. Say: that is an harmful thing for a husband to have sexual intercourse with his wife while she is going through her menses. Therefore keep away from women during menses and do not go near them until they have purified (themselves from menses and have taken a bath)... *Truly, Allah loves those who purify themselves* (by taking a bath and cleaning and washing their private parts and bodies) (Q. II: 222).

Taking bath is considered obligatory under the following conditions.

- Ejaculation or orgasm leading to fluid discharge whether in a state of sleep or wakefulness- in cases of men and women. However, if seminal fluid flows due to sickness or medication and not due to sexual urge, washing (*Ghusl*) is not obligatory. Likewise if a man or woman has a wet dream but finds no traces of emission, then bathing (*Ghusl*) is not necessary.

- Women also need not offer prayers during the period of their menses. The Apostle of Allah (peace & blessings of Allah be with him) is reported to have told Hadrat Fatimah bint Abi Hubaish: Leave *Salat* (prayers) during the days you menstruate, then take bath and offer *Salat* (prayer).

- If a believer dies, his body must be given a bath before burial.

- On his or her conversion to Islam, a neo-Muslim is required to take bath.
- A section of scholars have recommended that all Muslims must take bath before the Friday (*Jumu'ah*) prayers. According to a Tradition reported by Bukhari the Apostle of Allah (peace & blessings of Allah be with him) said: *Ghusl* on Friday is mandatory on all who have attained puberty.
- *Salat* is forbidden for those who happen to be in a state of *Janabah* (Sexual impurity)
- Similarly *Tawaf* (circumambulating) the holy Ka'bah is prohibited in a state of *Janabah*. According to Tirmidhi the Messenger of Allah (peace & blessings of Allah be with him) reportedly said: *Tawaf* around the House is *Salat*, except that Allah has permitted in it (ordinary) speech, so whoever speaks should speak nothing but good.
- It is not permitted to touch the Qur'an or carry it in a state of sexual impurity.
- One is not allowed to go to a mosque in a state of sexual impurity. As the holy Book says:

O you who believe! Approach not prayer when you are in a drunken state until you know (the meaning) *what you utter, nor when you are in a state of sexual impurity except when traveling on the road* (without sufficient water or just passing through mosque) *till you wash your whole body (Q. 4:43).*

Precepts Regarding Bath (*Ghusl*)

Under the Islamic Law (*Shari'ah*) two actions are necessary for taking bath. First, it is necessary to make an intention in the heart which distinguishes the prescribed *Ghusl* from ordinary bath. And secondly, all parts of the body should be washed. While taking a ritual bath it is best to observe the *Sunnah* of the holy Prophet (peace & blessings of Allah be with him):

- Begin by washing hands three times.
- Wash private parts of the body.
- Perform ablution (*Wudhu*) and thereafter wash the whole body beginning from the right side, then the left, ensuring that the water washes inaccessible parts such as inside of the ears, the hollow of the belly, between the toes etc.

According to a *Hadith* cited on the authority of Hadrat Ayesha: when the Prophet (peace & blessings of Allah be with him) used to take bath (in a state of sexual impurity) he would begin by washing both hands, then with his left hand he used to wash his private parts; thereafter he would perform *Wudhu*, like the *Wudhu* of *Salat*; then with water he would run his fingers through the roots of his hair until the water touched the scalp. Thereafter, he would pour water over his head three times, and then pour water over the rest of his body.

Desirable (*Mustahab*) Bath

Mustahab Ghusl is a bath that is considered praiseworthy and therefore worthy of rewards in the Hereafter. But for those who ignore such bath there is no blame and no punishment.

The Friday prayer bath (*Ghusl Jumuah*). The holy Prophet recommended bath before the Friday congregational prayers so that the Muslims attend it in the best conditions of cleanliness and purity.

According to a *Hadith* recorded by Imam Bukhari the Messenger of Allah is reported to have said:

- The *Ghusl* of Friday is obligatory for those who have attained puberty, and also cleaning of teeth by *Miswak* (tooth stick taken from the twigs of the Arak and other trees) and use of perfume, if available.

- *Ghusl* for the two Eid prayers.
- *Ghusl* is recommended for the one who has bathed a dead body. The Apostle of Allah is reported to have said: whoever washes a dead body should take a bath and whoever carries the dead body should take a bath *(At-Tirmidhi)*.
- Taking bath before entering in a state of *Ihram* for Hajj and *Umrah* is recommended by a majority of religious scholars.
- Bath is also recommended for those who enter the city of Makkah.

There is no difference between the bath of a man and a woman. The *Ghusl* of a woman is just like the *Ghusl* of a man. A woman need not undo her braids if the water reaches the roots of her hair. According to a *Hadith* recorded by Imam Muslim on the authority of Umm Salamah: A woman asked the holy Prophet: O Messenger of Allah! I am a woman who keeps the braids of her head tight. Do I have to undo it when performing a *Ghusl* in a state of *Janabah*? The Apostle of Allah (peace & blerssings of Allah be with him) is reported to have said that it was enough to pour three scoops of water over it, followed by pouring water over the whole body. After that purification is complete.

However, according to another *Hadith*, reported in the *Al-Mughni* of Ibn Qadamah, a woman should undo her braid for the *Ghusl* after menses.

Washing oneself in public bath is permitted provided on does not expose one's body to the others. *Hadith* recorded by Imam Muslim reported that the holy Prophet (peace & blessings of Allah be with him) said: A man should not look at another man's private parts nor a woman look at another woman's private parts.

However, it is considered necessary that a person should

perform ablution (*Wudhu*) along with the bath for his *Ghusl* to be complete.

Wiping (*Masah*) over a bandage At times it may not be possible for a person to wash his or her body due to injury illness or similar other reasons.

When a person has a wound or broken bone or other injuries and wants to perform ablution or bath and if he fears that washing the afflicted limb is likely to increase affliction, delay his recovery or any such thing; it is permitted to wrap the limb with a bandage and wipe over the whole bandage once during the course of ablution or *Ghusl*.

There is no requirement in the case of the bandage or cast that the person be in a state of purity when it was first applied, and there is no time limit on how long one can keep wiping over it. It is permitted to wipe over it during bath and ablution as long as the reason for doing so remains.

However the permission to wipe on the bandage ends when it is removed or when the injury heals so that there is no further need for wiping.

Tayammum
Purification with clean sand or clay under certain circumstances

Purification with sand or clay is permitted when water is insufficient or not available. The holy Qur'an asserts:

> And if you are unwell, or on a Journey, or if you return after the call of nature, or you have been in contact with women (by sexual relations) and you find no water, perform Tayammum with clean earth and rub therewith your faces and hands (Tayammum). Truly, Allah is Ever Oft-Pardoning, Oft-Forgiving (Q. 4:43).

The Apostle of Allah (peace & blessings of Allah be with

him) is reported to have said: Dust is a purifier for whoever does not find water, even if it were for ten years. (Abu Dawud) *Tayammum* is permissible as a substitute for ablution (*Wudhu*) or bath (*Ghusl*) under the following circumstances.

- *Tayammum* is allowed if one is wounded or sick and fears that use of water will aggravate illness or delay recovery.
- It is permissible if water is very cold (as in low temperature areas) and it is feared that its use could be harmful, and there are no means to warm it.
- *Tayammum* is allowed when water is nearby but the person fears for his life or honour or property or separation from his companions, or if an enemy is between him and water, (human or other) if he is imprisoned, or if there is no means to take water out of the well — in all these cases the availability of water is like it being unavailable. In the same manner if one fears being accused of something he is innocent of, due to performing a bath, then *Tayammum* is allowed.
- If some water is available but it is required for drinking, cooking, washing away impurity, or needed to be given to an animal; in such circumstances too *Tayammum* is permissible.

How to Perform *Tayammum*?

Tayammum can be performed with clean sand or mud or anything else which originates from the face of the earth such as pebbles etc.

The scholars of Arabic language agree that the word *Sayeed* used in the Qura'nic verse 43 of *Surah* 4 referring to *Tayammum*, means the face of the earth.

Before one proceeds to perform *Tayammum* It is important to make an intention of purification from a state of minor or major impurity. Then begin with the name of Allah by reciting *Bismillah*, then wipe the face and hands upto and including the wrist.

Tayammum is a substitute for ablution and bath when water is unavailable or insufficient. After a single *Tayammum* one is allowed to pray as many *Salat* as one intends to, obligatory or intentional. Hence *Tayammum* is exactly like ablution with water. In a *Hadith* recorded by Imam Ahmad, on the authority of Abu Zarr, the holy Prophet (peace & blessings of Allah be with him) is reported to have said:

The clean earth is a purifier for the Muslim, even if he cannot find water for ten years. But when he finds water he should use it for that is better.

Anything that nullifies *Wudhu* also nullifies *Tayammum*. Also the availability of water nullifies it, for those who made *Tayammum* due to its non-availability. However, if one performed *Salat* after *Tayammum* and then found water it is not required to repeat the *Salat*.

However, if neither water nor sand or mud is available a person is permitted to offer *Salat*. This opinion is based on the *Hadith* recorded by Imam Muslim and Imam An-Nawawi on the authority of Hadrat Ayesha that she had borrowed a necklace from her sister Asma' and it got lost on the way while Hadrat Ayesha was returning from an expedition along with the holy Prophet. Some companions went to look for it and around the time of prayers offered their *Salat* without ablution as there was no water around. On their return they told about it to the holy Prophet, who made no objection. It was at this time that the verse of *Tayammum* was revealed.

Precepts Regarding Menstruation

After attaining puberty women usually have menstruation (flowing out of blood from uterus) which lasts 6 to 7 days. when the flow of blood ceases, a woman should consider herself clean. (as elucidated by Imam ash-Shafeyi). If the colour of the blood is yellowish, pale or of muddy shade (between yellow and black) and it appears during the course of menstruation or in continuance of it, it should be treated as menstrual blood. However, if it appears after complete cessation of the normal coloured menstrual blood, then it should not be considered as menstruation.

The rules regarding menstruation also apply to post-partum bleeding (*Nifas*)

Restrictions on Menstruating Women and Those with Post-Partum Bleeding

Certain restrictions are placed on women who happen to be menstruating or who are going through post-partum bleeding. They cannot offer prayers (*Salat*). The prophet (peace & blessings of Allah be with him) is reported to have said: when menstruation begins, leave off *Salat*. Similarly *Tawaf* (circling) of the Ka'ba is prohibited. The Apostle of Allah reportedly said: Do everything that the *Hajj* pilgrim does, but do not perform circumambulation (*Tawaf*) of the House (*Ka'ba*) until you are purified. Fasting too is prohibited during days of menstruation and post-partum bleeding. Hadrat Ayesha is reported to have narrated: when we menstruated (during the lifetime of the Prophet) we were told to make up for the left fasting (of the month of *Ramadhan*) and we were not told to makeup for *Salat*.

Sitting in the mosque or at the place of Eid prayers is also prohibited.

It is also forbidden for the husband to have sex with a menstruating wife, as it is forbidden for her to allow it. The Holy Qur'an asserts:

> *They ask you concerning menstruation. Say: that is a harmful thing for a husband to have sexual intercourse with his wife while she is having her menses; therefore keep away from women during menses and go not unto*

them till they have purified (from menses and have taken a bath). *(Q. 2:222)*

In a Tradition reported by Imam Muslim, the Apostle of Allah (peace & blessings of Allah be with him) is reported to have remarked:

You may do everything with them (your menstruating wives) except intercourse.

Imam An-Nawawi reported from Imam Ash-Shafeyi that: Whoever does that (has intercourse with his menstruating wife) has committed a major sin and whoever says that intercourse with a menstruating woman is legal should be ruled a disbeliever.

Many religious scholars are of the opinion that it is better for a menstruating woman not to recite the holy Qur'an orally. However listening to the recitation of the Qur'an is not prohibited. In such a state reciting *Allahu-Akbar*, or *Subhan Allah* or *Alhamdu-Lillah* or *Bismillah* or making supplications or saying *Ameen*, where it is necessary, is permitted. Reading *Hadith* or *Fiqh* is also allowed.

Rules Regarding *Istihadhah*

Some women have vaginal bleeding (*Istihadhah*) that is different from menstruation or bleeding of the child birth. There is no difference between a woman beset by *Istihadhah* and a woman whose menstruation has stopped, except the following:

- During *Istihadhah* if a woman wants to perform *Wudhu* she is required to wash blood from her vaginal area then use a menstrual pad or cover the area with a clean cloth and cotton. Any blood flowing out thereafter is of no account.

- And she must perform ablution for every obligatory prayer (*Fard Salat*).

According to a *Hadith* recorded by Imam Bukhari, the holy prophet is reported to have said: perform *Wudhu* for every *Salat*.

Precepts Regarding Ablution (*Wudhu*)

Since there is no prayer without purification of the body the importance of ablution, in addition to washing the body, is emphasized by the holy Prophet (peace & blessings of Allah be with him) and all eminent religious scholars of Islam.

The holy Qur'an reads: *O you who believe! When you intend to offer prayer, wash your faces and your hands* (forearms) *upto the elbows, rub your heads* (by passing wet hands over your head) *and* (wash) *your feet upto the ankles* (Q. V:6).

According to a Tradition recorded by Imam Muslim on the authority of Abu Hurayra, the Apostle of Allah (peace & blessings of Allah be with him) said: Allah does not accept prayer of a person who is not in a state of *Wudhu*; until *Wudhu* is performed.

The first step to be taken before ablution (*Wudhu*) is performed is to make an intention with in the heart and begin in the name of Allah by reciting *Bismillah* (I begin with the name of Allah).

Tirmidhi has recorded a *Hadith* on the authority of Sayeed ibn Zaid according to which the Messenger of Allah (peace & blessings of Allah be with him) said:

Whoever does not recite *Bismillah* before *Wudhu*, his *Wudhu* is not complete.

Step two is to wash your hands three times upto the wrists, rinse mouth with water and draw water inside the nose upto the nose bone — three times.

Step three: wash your face (from ear to ear and forehead to chin) three times.

Step four: beginning with the right hand, wash your forearms upto and including the elbow, three times.

Step five: wipe your wet hands over hair or scalp (all of it) and wipe the inside and back of the ears with the forefingers and the thumb.

Step Six: Wash the feet with your left hand upto and including the ankles, three times; beginning with the right foot.

No part of the body over which *Wudhu* is performed should be left dry.

Abu Dawud has reported from Laqeeth ibn Sabra that the holy prophet used to comb his beard with his wet hands and used to wash spaces between fingers of his hands and fingers of his feet.

The hoy Prophet (peace & blessings of Allah be with him) also recommended cleaning of teeth by *miswak* (took stick) before bath and ablution. Hadrat Ayesha is reported by Imam Ahmed as having said that the Messenger of Allah (peace & blessings of Allah be with him) stated that *Miswak* keeps the mouth clean and is a means of seeking pleasure of Allah.

Step Seven: After ablution say: I bear witness that none has the right to be worshiped but Allah Alone and without partners, and I bear witness that Muhammad is His slave and His Messenger.

According to a Tradition reported by Imam Muslim on the authority of Umar the holy Prophet (peace & blessings of Allah be with him) said: All the eight gates of Paradise are opened for the believer when, after performing *Wudhu* completely, a believer recites the following supplication:

I testify that there is no one worthy of worship but Allah and Muhammad is the servant and Messenger of Allah.

Tirmidhi has added the following words to this supplication:

O' Allah include me among those who repent and those who keep themselves pure.

Things That Nullify *Wudhu*

Certain things nullify ablution such as:

- Things coming out of the private parts of the body including urine, excrement, semen and gas; whether it escapes silently or otherwise. Imam Muslim has reported the Mesenger of Allah (peace & blessings of Allah be with him) as having said: Allah will not accept prayer (*Salat*) of anyone of you if he (or she) passes out anything from his private parts until he (or she) performs *Wudhu* (ablution).

- The leaking of *Madhyi* or *Wadyi*; *Madhyi* is prostatic fluid which seeps out during sexual arousal, before ejaculation. And *Wadyi* is a fluid that seeps out after urine without any accompanying sexual arousal (usually due to some illness). When asked what one should do if *Madhyi* is excreted, the holy Prophet (peace & blessings of Allah be with him) is reported to have said:

He (or she) should wash his (or her) sex organ and perform *Wudhu*.

- Deep sleep also nullifies *Wudhu*. This is the kind of sleep where no trace of wakeful consciousness remains.

- Loss of consciousness also nullifies *Wudhu*. It may be due to insanity or fainting, drunkenness or sedation.

- Touching one's private parts without any intervening barrier (of clothes etc.) also nullifies *Wudhu*. Imam Bukhari and Tirmidhi have reported the Messenger of Allah as saying: whoever touches his (sex) organ should not pray until he performs ablution (*Wudhu*).

Things That Do Not Nullify Ablution

- Touching a woman, that is, skin to skin contact, does not nullify *Wudhu*.

  Hadrat Ayesha is reported to have said that: I used to sleep in front of the Prophet and my feet would be between him and the *Qiblah* (direction of the Ka'ba), so whenever he prostrated his hands would brush the side of my feet.

- The flow of blood from any part of the body other than the vagina does not nullify *Wudhu*. Bukhari has reported Hadrat Hasan as having said that the Muslims used to continue to pray while they had wounds.

- Vomit, enough to fill the mouth or less, does not nullify *Wudhu*.

- State of Doubt regarding excretion of stool, urine gas etc. from private parts after performing ablution (*Wudhu*) does not nullify it. For certain knowledge cannot be superseded by uncertainty. On the contrary, if one is sure of excretion then *Wudhu* is nullified.

- Laughing aloud during *Salat* does not nullify *Wudhu*. There is a weak *Hadith* which states that laughing aloud nullifies *Wudhu*, but a week *Hadith* cannot establish a point of law.

- Giving bath to a deadbody does not require a person to perform ablution again. In fact, in view of the available evidence on this matter, it may be said that *Wudhu* in such situation is recommended but not necessary.

- Dozing off without back rest does not invalidate *Wudhu*.

Abu Dawud has quoted Anas ibn Malik that when the holy Prophet was alive the companions while waiting for the *Isha* prayers dozed off and performed prayer without performing ablution again.

After the performing of *Wudhu* a believer is in a state of prayer and should therefore not indulge in absurd talk and useless acts. Imam Ahmad has reported a Tradition on the authority of Ka'b ibn Ujrah that the holy Prophet said: After performing *Wudhu* when you proceed towards the mosque do not twine your fingers; for after *Wudhu* you are in a state of prayer.

After performing *Wudhu* or *Ghusl* (ablution or bath) one may or may not wipe water from the body with a cloth or towel:

Tirmidhi has reported from Hadrat Ayesha that the holy Prophet used a piece of cloth to dry the parts of the body over which *Wudhu* was performed.

Also one many wash once, twice or thrice the parts of the body where *Wudhu* is to be performed. However it is not recommended to wash more than three times. Imam Muslim has reported from Ibn Abbas that the holy Prophet performed ablution by washing his parts of the body only once.

Imam Bukhari has reported from Abdullah ibn Zaid that the holy Prophet washed part of his body twice only during ablution.

Imam Ahmad has reported from Amr ibn Shoaib that Abdullah ibn Amr ibn A'as said that a villager inquired from the Messenger of Allah (peace & blessings of Allah be with him) about the mode of performing ablution. The holy Prophet demonstrated by washing parts of the body three times and said: This is the way to perform *Wudhu*. Whoever washes these parts more than this has committed wrong, excess and outrage.

It is also, reported that several prayers can be performed with one *Wudhu*, if it has not been nullified. Imam Muslim has reported from Buraidah that on the day of the conquest of Makka the Messenger of Allah (peace & blessings of Allah be with him) performed several prayers with one *Wudhu*.

Excellence of *Wudhu*

Ablution before every prayer is not only a means of purification of the body and the soul but has many concealed, and unknown benefits. One such blessing of *Wudhu* is reported by Abu Hurayra (recorded by Imam Muslim) that the Messenger of Allah (peace & blessings of Allah be with him) said: My fountain (in paradise) is bigger than the distance between Aden and Ayla. Its water is whiter than snow and sweeter than honey and milk. (On the Day of Reckoning) I shall prevent other people (of other communities) from approaching the fountain. The companions enquired: O Messenger of Allah! would you recognize us among other people on that Day? The holy prophet (peace & blessings of Allah be with him) said: yes due to *Wudhu* your hands and feet would be so bright that no other people would have such signs.

8
PURIFICATION OF THE SOUL

PURIFICATION OF THE SOUL

Best Sustenance for the Heart is Faith;
And the Best Medicine is the Qur'an

Acts of purification, cleanliness, of *Ghusl* (bathing) and ablution (*Wudhu*) are meant for the cleanliness of the body and purification of the spirit. The purity of one's heart is, however, far more important than that of the body. Well being of the heart ensures both a fortunate life in this world and eternal bliss in the hereafter.

The acts of obedience (to the commands of Allah) are indispensable to the well being of the heart. Remembrance of Allah, recitation of the holy Qur'an, seeking forgiveness of Allah, invoking blessings of Allah and peace on the holy prophet (peace & blessings of Allah be with him) and praying at night, in addition to the obligatory prayers, are some of the most significant acts for the purification of the heart.

But one must remember that the holy Prophet had said: Actions are only by intention, and every person shall only have what he (or she) intended. According to Imam Ash-Shafeyi this *Hadith* is a third of all knowledge. It implies that deeds which are performed in accordance with the *Sunnah* are only acceptable and rewarded if the intention behind them happens to be sincere.

The holy Prophet (peace & blessings of Allah be with him) had said: *'Actions depend upon their outcome.'* Many small actions are made great by the intentions behind them. Many great actions, on the other hand, are made small because the intention behind them is lacking.

Umar ibn al-Khattab (may Allah be pleased with him) is reported to have said: The best acts are doing what Allah has commanded; staying away from what Allah has forbidden, and having sincere intentions towards whatever Allah has required of us.

Similarly Yahya ibn Abu Kathir said:

Learn about intentions, for their importance is greater than the importance of actions.

And the holy Qur'an reads:

The Day (Day of Reckoning) *on which neither wealth nor sons will be of any use, except for whoever brings to Allah a sound heart (Q. 26: 88-89)*

The sound heart (*Qalb-e-Salim*) is a heart cleansed from any passion that challenges what Allah commands, or disputes what He forbids. It is free from any impulses which contradict His good.

As a result its services are exclusively reserved for Allah, willingly and lovingly, with total reliance, relating all matters to Him, in fear, hope and sincere dedication.

A dead heart, on the other hand, clings to its lusts and desires. Its whims are its *imam*; it lust is its guide. Its ignorance its leader. It is immersed in its concerns with worldly objectives. It is intoxicated with its own fancies and it loves for fleeting pleasures. It is a heart that is deaf and blind to righteousness. It is reported on the authority of Abu Darda that the Prophet said: 'Your love for something makes you blind and deaf.'

A sick heart contains illness as well as life. It is sustained by both as it follows whichever of the two manages to dominate it. It has love for Allah, or fear of Allah, sincerity and reliance on Him. At the same time, it has a craving for lust and pleasures of this worldly life. It is full of self-admiration, which can lead to self-destruction.

The first heart is alive, submitted to Allah, humble, sensitive and aware; the second is feeble and dead; the third wavers between safety and ruin. The more diseased the heart is, the more it desires the world and its pleasures.

The most beneficial sustenance for the heart is faith and the best medicine is the Qur'an. The healthy heart continues to trouble its owner until he or she returns to Allah and is at peace with Him, and joins Him.

Conversely, all acts of disobedience are poison to the heart and lead to sickness and ruin. Whoever is concerned with the health and life of his heart, must rid it of the effects of the poison of temptation, lust and worldly desires. Some of the important poisons that pose great risk to the health of the heart are useless talking, unrestrained glances, love for food and drink and keeping bad company.

It is reported on the authority of Anas ibn Malik that the Messenger of Allah (peace & blessings of Allah be with him) said:

The faith of a servant is not right until his heart is right and his heart is not right until his tongue is right.

In the light of this *Hadith* it has been observed that purification of faith is conditional on the purification of the heart, and purification of the heart depends on the purification of the tongue.

In a *Hadith* reported by Tirmidhi on the authority of Ibn Umar it is said: Do not talk excessively without remembering Allah, because such excessive talk without the mention of Allah causes the heart to harden, and the person farthest from Allah is a person with a hard heart. *(Tirmidhi, Kitab az-Zuhud 7/92).*

In another *Hadith* related on the authority of Mu'adh the holy Prophet (peace & blessings of Allah be with him) is reported to have said:

Is there anything more than the harvest of the tongue that throws people on their faces into the fire (of Hell). *(Sahih Hadith, At-Tirmidhi)*

A person, through his actions and words, sows the seeds of either good or evil. On the Day of Reckoning he harvests their fruit.

Those who sow the seeds of good words and deeds harvest honour and blessings; those who sow the seeds of evil words and deeds reap only regret and remorse.

According to Abu Hurayra the Messenger of Allah (peace & blessings of Allah be with him) said: the servant speaks words, the consequences of which he does not realize, and for which he is thrown into the depths of the fires (of Hell) further than the distance between the east and the west. *(Bukhari, Kitab ar Riqaq)*

Therefore the prophet cautioned the Muslims to either speak good or remain silent. *(Muslim, Kitab al Iman 2/18)*

The Muslims are therefore advised to enjoin the good and forbid the evil. For whoever cannot hold his tongue cannot understand his *Deen* (faith). Backbiting, gossiping, obscene talk, hypocritical conversation, showing off, quarrelling, lying, mockery, derision, falsehood and other such forbidden things are to be avoided at all times.

There is a direct connection between the eyes and the heart of a human. If the eyes are corrupted then the heart follows suit. Staring and gazing without restraint is considered to be disobedience to Allah.

A righteous person said: whoever enriches his outwards behaviour by following the *Sunnah*, and makes his inward soul wealthy through contemplation and averts his gaze away from looking at what is forbidden, and avoids things of dubious nature, and feeds solely on what is licit (*halal*) — His inner sight will never falter. And when the heart is a light, countless goods comes to it from all directions. If it is dark, then clouds of evil and afflictions come from all directions to cover it up.

Similarly, consumption of small quantity of food guarantees tenderness of the heart, strength of the intellect, humility of the self, weakness of desires and gentleness of temperament. Conversely excessive eating result in opposite qualities.

According to a *Hadith* reported by Imam Ahmed the Messenger of Allah said:

The son of Adam fills no vessel displeasing to Allah than his stomach. A few morsels should be enough for him to preserve his strength. If he must fill it, then he should allow a third (of space) for his food, a third for his drink, and leave a third empty for easy breathing.

Ibrahim ibn Adham is reported to have said that anyone who controls his stomach is in control of his *Deen*, and anyone who controls his hunger is in control of good behaviour. Disobedience to Allah is nearest to a person who is satisfied with a full stomach.

Whoever safeguards against the evils of over filling his stomach has prevented great evil.

Acts of obedience are essential for the well being of the heart, in the same way that food and drink are necessary for the nourishment of the body.

Surely in Remembrance of Allah Do Hearts Find Rest (Q.13:28)

Remembrance of Allah is sustenance for the heart as well as the spirit. According to Ibn Taimiyya: Remembrance of Allah is to the heart what water is to fish. Such an act adorns the heart with delight, fills it with light and blesses the believer with dignity, gentleness and freshness.:

The Holy Qur'an proclaims:

So remember Me (and) I will remember you (Q. 2: 152) and *Remembrance of Allah is greatest (Q. 29: 45)*

Abu Musa reported that the Messenger of Allah (peace & blessings of Allah be with him) said: The difference between the one who remembers his Lord and the one who does not is like the difference between the living and the dead *(Bukhari, Kitab ad-Da'wat 11/208)*

Although remembrance is one of the easiest form of worship the blessings and rewards that it brings cannot be achieved by any other means.

Abu Hurayra reported that the Messenger of Allah said:

Whoever recites the words: *'There is no deity but Allah, the One, having no partner with Him. Sovereignty belongs to him and All praise is due to Him, and He is powerful over everything'*, one hundred times everyday, there is a reward (for him or her) equal to freeing ten slaves and a hundred good actions are recorded (in his or her) account and a hundred wrong actions are blotted out from his record. *(Al-Bukhari Kitab ad-Da'wat 11/201)*

Remembrance of Allah is a remedy for hard hearts, sick hearts and dead hearts. Whoever has the gates of remembrance opened to him has an opening to his Lord and if one finds Allah, one has found everything. And if the opportunity is missed during a life time one has missed everything. *'Surely in the remembrance of Allah do hearts find rest' (Q. 13:28)*.

The best kind of remembrance is to recite the Book of Allah because it contains remedies to cure the heart from all illness. It is declared to be a *'healing and mercy for those who believe'* *(Q. 17:82);* *'a protection from your Lord and a healing for what is in your hearts, and for those who believe in guidance and mercy* *(Q. 10: 57).*

The holy Qur'an is a cure from the desires and doubt. It contains wisdom and good counsel and it enables its reader to distinguish the right from the wrong. Above all, the holy Book brings the servant nearer to the Lord.

Surely those of His Servants, who know, Fear Allah *(Q.35:28)*

Love of Allah gives life to the heart and sustains the soul. The heart experiences no pleasure, nor feels any joy, if it does not contain the love of Allah.

To love Allah is to be with Him always, to remember Him continuously with longing. The most beneficial, the most sincere, most elevated and most exalted form of love is most certainly the love of the One for Whom hearts were created to love, and for Whom creation was brought into existence to adore. Allah is the One towards Whom hearts turn in love, exaltation, glorification, humility, submission and worship.

At the same time a believer cannot be devoid of the fear of Allah. Allah has commanded His servants to fear Him and has made belief conditional upon fear. Allah proclaims: **Fear Me if you are believers.** *(Q. 3: 175)*

Guidance, mercy, knowledge, and acceptance is granted to those who fear Allah. Lack of fear leads to negligence and heedlessness and boldness in committing sins. The fear of accountability in the court of the Lord, the fear of the punishments of Hell, is likely to deter a believer from disobedience and sin. Those who do not believe in the rewards and punishments on the Day of Reckoning do not fear Allah and therefore have no hope of salvation.

Fear tames the limbs and fills the heart with submission, humility and tranquility. Fear takes away arrogance, hatred and envy from the heart. According to *Sahih* of Tirmidhi the Prophet (peace & blessings of Allah be with him) is reported to have said:

No believer who has wept from the fear of Allah, will ever enter the Fire (of Hell) unless milk returns back to its udder.

Allah, the Most High, says in the holy Book:

Surely those who live in awe of fear of their Lord, and those who believe in the signs of their Lord, and those who do not associate partners with their Lord in their worship, and those who give what they gave with fear in their hearts because they are returning to their Lord — it is these who hasten to do good, and in this they are foremost (Q. 23: 57-61)

And these people, according to the Holy Prophet, are the ones who regularly fast and pray and give *Zakat* and fear that their good deeds may not be accepted (it is those who hasten to do good). *(Sahih, at-Tirmidhi Kitab al-Tafseer 9/19).*

And Seek Forgiveness of Allah

And whoever does evil, or wrongs his own soul, but afterwards seeks Allah's forgiveness, will find *Allah is Forgiving, Compassionate (Q. 4: 110)* An-Numan ibn Bashir reported that the Messenger of Allah said: supplication is worship itself. Then he recited the following verse:

And your Lord has said: *'call on Me- I will answer you'*. Surely those who are too arrogant to worship Me will enter Hell in humiliation. *(Q. 40: 60)*

According to a *Hadith* related by Abu Hurayra the Messenger of Allah said: whoever does not supplicate to Allah, invokes His wrath. *(Tirmidhi, Kitab al-Da'wat 9/313)*

Supplication to Allah can be made at all times but certain times are considered auspicious such as the early morning hours, Friday, month of Ramadan and the day of Arafat.

Abu Hurayra reported that the Messenger of Allah said: A servant is nearest to his Lord when he is in prostration, so increase your supplication when in prostration *(Muslim, kitab as Salah 4/200)*

In another *Hadith* reported by Dawud *(Kitab as Salah 2/224)* the holy Prophet said: supplication made during the time between *Adhan* and *Iqama* is never made in vain. And it is reported on the authority of Anas ibn Malik that the Apostle of Allah said:

Do not give up supplicating, for no one who supplicates is ruined. *(ibn Hibban, p596)*

Whoever does not supplicate to Allah invokes His wrath *(Ibn Majah, Kitab ad-Dua 2/1258)*

Allah likes those who seek His forgiveness: '*And seek forgiveness of Allah; surely Allah is Forgiving, Compassionate (Q. 73: 20)*

Seeking forgiveness is similar to supplication to Allah. Seeking forgiveness is associated with repentance, in which case it takes the form of asking for forgiveness with the tongue. Repentance is turning away from wrong actions in word and deed. Forgiveness, if sought directly from a heart troubled by wrong actions, or made during auspicious times may be granted by Allah to a sincere supplicant.

Al-Hasan is reported to have said that Allah's forgiveness should be frequently sought everywhere and at all times; for you never know when you will be granted His forgiveness.

As reported by Abu Hurayra, the Messenger of Allah said that he (the Prophet) supplicated for Allah's forgiveness and turned to Him in repentance more than seventy times a day. *(Al-Bukhari, Kitab ad-Da'wat 11/101)*

Turning in Repentance is the Beginning of the servant and his End

And those who do not turn in repentance are indeed wrongdoers (Q. 49:11)

Turning in repentance is the beginning of the servant and his end. A sincere seeker of Allah should never abandon repentance; he should continue to do so until his last breath.

And turn to Allah altogether, O you who believe, so that you may succeed (Q. 24: 31)

Allah has made success conditional on repentance. The only hope for success for the believers lie in turning to Him in repentance. Allah calls those who do not turn to Him in repentance as wrongdoers and transgressors, and says that no one is more of a wrongdoer than such a person, because of his ignorance of his Lord and of the rights that are due to Him.

Repentance is valid only if a person feels regret for his sins, abandons wrong actions and resolves never to repeat them.

For repentance to be true and sincere it must be free from deceit, defects and corruption. Sincere repentance is what purifies the soul.

Allah Most High says: *O you who believe, turn to Allah with sincere repentance so that your Lord may free you from your bad deeds and bring you into Gardens underneath which rivers flow, on the Day when Allah will not disgrace the Prophet and those who believe with him (Q 66: 8)*

The servant is oft-repentant and Allah is Oft-Forgiving. The repentance of the servant is his turning back to his Lord after his having turned away.

Whoever turns in repentance and does good has truly turned to Allah in true repentance (Q. 25: 71)

Reliance on Allah is an Essential act of Faith

'Truly My Mercy prevails over My wrath'

If a believer sows the seeds of belief, and waters them with obedience to and worship of Allah, and purifies his heart of bad elements, and than waits for the blessings from Allah, in the form of His keeping him steadfast in that state until his death, and then granting him an excellent end and His forgiveness — then his waiting is truly hoping for the best.

Allah, Most High, says in His Book: *surely those who believe and those who make Hijra (emigrate) and strive in the way of Allah, these are the ones who have hope of mercy of Allah; and Allah is Forgiving, Compassionate. (Q. 2: 218)*

Such people are worthy of hoping for Allah's mercy. But others can be hopeful too. The one who hopes guides himself to obedience of Allah.

It is reported or the authority of Anas that he heard the Messenger of Allah say: Allah has said: *O' son of Adam, as long as you call on Me and ask of Me, I will forgive you for what you have done, and I shall not mind. O son of Adam, were your sins to reach the clouds of sky and were you then to ask forgiveness of Me, I would forgive you.*

O son of Adam, were you to come to Me with sins nearly as great as the earth, and were you then to face Me without having associated anything with Me, I would bring you for-giveness nearly as great as it.' (At-Tirmidhi, Kitab ad-Da'wat 9/524)

According to Sayeed Ibn Zubayr: Reliance on Allah in an essential part of faith.

Reliance on Allah is the sincere dependence of the heart on Allah in the endeavors of the believer in pursuing his interests and safeguarding himself against anything that may be harmful to his well-being in this life and in the hereafter.

A person who relies on Allah and fears him will find that these two qualities are sufficient for him in worldly affairs and in affairs of his *Deen*.

Possessing the state of reliance on Allah, however, does not prevent the believer from utilizing the ways and means which Allah has decreed for His creation. These are His laws and He has commanded humans to use ways and means, while at the same time He has instructed believers to rely on Him. Endeavouring to make use of the ways and means in His universe with limbs is obedience, and relying on Him in the hearts is faith in Him. Ignoring ways and means is doubting the need for the *Shariah* of Islam, while trusting entirely in ways and means is doubting the Reality of *Tawheed* (the existence of One Allah).

And Allah Loves those who Persevere

Success in this life and in the hereafter is conditional on perseverance and righteousness. And *Allah loves those who persevere.* (Q. 3: 146)

Perseverance is standing firm and remaining courteous when affliction strikes, and remaining content in adversities, without showing any sign of complaint.

In the Holy Book Allah has praised those who persevere and has promised them endless rewards and supports such believers with His guidance, might and clear victory. He says: **And be patient – surely Allah is with those who are patient** (Q. 8: 46)

Perseverance is a true attribute of a believer. It is the pillar that supports his faith, without which he may not remain upright. Whoever has no perseverance has no faith, or his faith is weak; such a person worships Allah half-heartedly: if he succeeds in life, gets his hearts desire he is reassured in his belief, but if he faces setbacks and failures then he turns away from Allah and thereby loses everything in this life and in the hereafter. Blessings and Mercy of Allah are promised to those who persevere in adversities:

And give good news to those who persevere, those who say, when a misfortune strickes them, "Surely we come from Allah and surely to Him we return"; these are the ones on whom blessings from their Lord descend, and mercy, and these are the ones who are rightly guided (Q. 2: 153-157).

Perseverance and gratitude are two elements of faith, whoever is concerned about the well being of his soul — desiring its salvation and hoping for its good fortune — must cultivate the virtues of perseverance and gratitude.

Gratitude is a matter for the heart, the tongue and the limbs. The heart knows and loves Allah; tongue praises and thanks Him and the limbs obey Him.

Gratitude is linked with belief. Allah says that He does not need to punish His creatures if they thank Him and believe in Him:

What has Allah to do with punishing you, if you are grateful and you believe; (Q. 4: 147).

Allah has granted so many blessings on humans, inspite of their disobedience, that it is impossible for us to count them. Yet humans remain heedless and most of us do not care to thank Him enough.

And only a few of My servants are grateful (Q. 34: 13).

When the Messenger of Allah was asked why he stayed up in prayer all night until his feet swelled up, when Allah has forgiven all his past and future wrong actions; the holy Prophet replied: should I not still be a grateful servant *(Bukhari, Kitab at-Tahajjud 3/14)*

The Apostle of Allah once told Muadh.

By Allah, you are dear to Me! So do not forget to say at the end of each prayer, O Allah! Help me in remembering You, in being grateful to You and in serving You well. *(Ahmad, al-Musnad 5/245)*

Gratitude towards Allah is linked to Allah's generosity and it increases His generosity. Ali Ibn Talib is reported to have told a man from the tribe of Hamazan; Allah's generosity is connected to gratitude, and gratitude is linked to increase in His generosity. The generosity of Allah will not stop increasing unless the gratitude of His servant ceases. And the holy Book reads:

And speak about the blessings of your Lord (Q. 93: 11).

For speaking about His generosity frequently is an expression of gratitude towards Him. Yet however grateful a believer may be, he can never be grateful enough for Allah's blessings are vast and countless.

While patience is a duty that a believer must fulfill, being content is a praiseworthy quality. It involves feeling at ease in accepting the Divine Decree. Being content alleviates suffering by reason of the immersion of the heart in the spirit of certainty and knowledge.

According to Ibn Masud: Allah in His justice and wisdom, placed joy in certainly and contentment, and placed sadness and sorrow in doubt and discontentment.

Whoever is content with what he has, Allah will make it enough for him and bless it; and whoever is not content, Allah will neither make it enough for him nor bless it, Al-Hasan al-Basri is reported to have said.

Abd al wahid ibn Zayd said: Being content is the greatest door to Allah, the Garden of this life, and a place of rest for the worshippers.

And it is reported on the authority of Anas ibn Malik that the Apostle of Allah said: when Allah loves someone then He tests him: as for whoever is content — Allah will be pleased with him; and for whoever is discontented — Allah will be displeased with him. *(At-Tirmidhi Kitab az-zuhud 7/77)*

According to Al-Fudayl: The one who is content is the one who lives simply, and it is he who is rich. The one who has attained real faith, who trusts in Allah in all his affairs, and is content with what He provides for him, and remains unattached to the creation, out of fear and hope — and by so doing finds that pursuing worldly gains is not worthwhile —

has attained the benefits of simplicity. He is the richest of people, even though he may not possess a thing in this world.

Hadrat Ali reportedly said that 'whoever lives simply in this world finds misfortune easy to endure'.

The life of this world is a test for the humans a test of their conduct and their deeds. It is also an opportunity for making provision for the life in the hereafter. Allah says in the Qur'an:

Surely we have put what is on the earth as a glittering show so that we may test them, as to which of them have the best actions (Q. 18: 7)

That is why Abu Sufiyan ar Rayini said: Everything you do in this world with the intention of making a profit is blameworthy, and everything you do in order to profit in the next world has nothing to do with this world.

Love for this worldly life is considered an evil for it ruins the faith of the people in many ways. The least of its evils is that it distracts people from the remembrance and love of Allah. The one who loves the life of this world suffers in this world, in his grave and on the Day of Reckoning.

The journey of those who seek Allah ends with them overcoming their selves, because whoever triumphs over his self succeeds and wins, and whoever allows his self to triumph over him loses.

Allah, Most High, has warned:

Then as for whoever exceeded the limits and preferred the life of this world, surely his abode will be the fire (of Hell); *and for whoever feared to stand before his Lord and restrained the desires of himself, surely his abode will be the Garden (Q. 79: 37-40).*

The self stands between the heart and reaching Him. Only the silencing of the self-by turning away from it and ignoring its whims And overcoming it — can lead a person into the domain of Allah and make it possible to reach Him.

In the Qur'an Allah has described three states of the self: the self at peace, the reproachful self and the self that urges evil.

The peace that comes with *Ihsan*, that is the state of being absolutely sincere to Allah in oneself, springs from reassuring familiarity with the decree of Allah, which is reflected in submission, sincerity and worship.

The reproachful self finds no rest in any situation. It often changes, remembers and forgets, submits and evades, loves and hates, accepts and rejects, obeys and rebels.

Another self urges evil. By its very nature it guides its owner towards wrong actions. No one can be rid of its evil without help from Allah.

The self at peace has an angel to help it and guide it. The self that urges evil has Satan as its ally.

Imam Ahmad has related on the authority of Umar ibn al-Khattab that the Apostle of Allah said: The intelligent person is the one who brings his self to account and acts in preparation for what lies beyond his death; and the foolish person is the one who abandons himself to his desires and cravings and expects Allah to fulfil his futile wishes. *(Tirmidhi, Kitab Sifat al-Qiyamah).*

A believer should be able to judge his actions before he is judged on the Day of Reckoning. Al-Hasan said: A believer is responsible for his self, and he brings it to account in order to please Allah. Judgement will be lighter on the Day of Reckoning for those who have brought themselves to account in this life, but it will be severe for the people who did not prepare for it by bringing their selves to account beforehand.

A believer should first bring his self to account as regards his obligatory acts of worship. It he finds himself lacking in it, then he should hasten to rectify the situation.

Next a believer should bring himself to account regarding

acts that are forbidden. And turn in repentance if he discovers his misdeeds and seek Allah's forgiveness, and do good deeds in order to eradicate the bad deeds.

Similarly the self should be accounted for with regard to matters in which it has been negligent, for the words spoken, for the steps his feet have taken, and so on.

Finally the rights of Allah must be acknowledged such as the right to be constantly remembered, obeyed and thanked. This is important as it makes the believer detest his self and frees him from arrogance and being self-satisfied with his actions. Such realization is likely to open the doors of submission and humility for him and is likely to result in the purification of his soul by the Grace, Generosity and Mercy of Allah.

REFERENCES

Azad, Abul kalam. Tarjuman al Quran; Syed Abdul Lateef (trans.), N
Gibbon, HAR. Whither Islam ?
Asad, Muhammad, *The Road to Mecca*
Ali, Syed Amir, *The Spirit of Islam*, London 1920
Sardar Ziauddin, *The Future of Islamic Civilization*, London 1989.
Al-Isfahani, Raghib. *Mufradat Gharaib al-Qur'an*, Cario, 1325 AH, Vol. I
Majah, Ibn. *Kitab al-Fitun*
Ibn Hanbal, Ahmad. *Musnad* vol. VI
Smith, Bosworth. *Muhammad and Muhammadanism*, London, 1870
Maududi, Sayyid Abu al-A'la. *Al-Jihad fi al-Islam*, Lahore, 1948
Bukhari, *Kitab al-Muzalim wa al-Ga'saba*, Vol. II
Bukhari, *Kitab al-Jihad wa al-Siyar* Vol. III
Al-Asqalani, ibn Hajar, *Fath al-Bari, Kitab al Jihad*. Vol. VI
Abu Dawud, *Kitab al-Jihad*, Karachi, 1953. Vol. II
Je Geo, M. J. (ed.) Al-Tabari, *Tarikh al-Rasul wa al-Muluk*, 1580, Vol. IV
Encyclopaedia Britannica, London, Vol. XXIII (WAR).
Zidan, Ahmad (Tr.), *Sahih Muslim*, Kuala Lampur, 2002
Ali, A. Y., *The meaning of the Illustrious Qur'an,* IBS, New Delhi
Sahih, an-Nisai, Kitab al-Jihad IBS, 2003
Sahih, ibn Majah
Al-Bukhari, Kitab al Qadr
Muslim, Kitab at-Tahara
Al-Bukhari, Kitab ar-Riqaq
Muslim, Kitab al-Iman.
At-Tirmidhi, Kitab az-Zuhd
Bukhari, Kitab ad-Da'wat
Muslim, Kitab adh-Dhikr wa'd-Dua
At-Tirmidhi, Kitab ad-Da'wat
Al-Bukhari, Kitab at-Tawhid
Muslim, Kitab al-Iman
Muslim, Kitab as-Salah
Hasan, at-Tirmidhi, Kitab al Witr
Al Bukhari, Kitab at-Tahajjud
Al Bukhari, Kitab az-Zakat
Hasan, ibn Majah, Kitab az-Zuhud